Prostitution in Victorian Colchester

Prostitution in Victorian Colchester
Controlling the Uncontrollable

Jane Pearson and Maria Rayner

Essex Publications
an imprint of
University of Hertfordshire Press

First published in Great Britain in 2018 by
Essex Publications
an imprint of
University of Hertfordshire Press
College Lane
Hatfield
Hertfordshire
AL10 9AB

© Copyright Jane Pearson and Maria Rayner 2018

The right of Jane Pearson and Maria Rayner to be identified as the authors of this work has been asserted by them in accordance with the Copyright, Designs and Patents Act 1988.

All rights reserved. No part of this book may be reproduced or utilized in any form or by any means, electronic or mechanical, including photocopying, recording or by any information storage and retrieval system, without permission in writing from the publisher.

British Library Cataloguing in Publication Data
A catalogue record for this book is available from the British Library

ISBN 978-1-909291-97-3

Design by Arthouse Publishing Solutions Ltd
Printed in Great Britain by Hobbs the Printers Ltd

Dedication

Some are born to sweet delight
Some are born to endless night.

(William Blake, *Auguries of Innocence*)

This book is dedicated to Maria Rayner's grandmothers, Sylvia Lambert and Florence Andrews. Sylvia hired the social club of the printing firm Spottiswoode, Ballantyne & Co in Port Lane, Colchester to celebrate her daughter's wedding on 26 December 1956. Standing in the club's kitchen peeling potatoes for the wedding breakfast, Sylvia noticed that the windows were barred. She commented to Maria's other grandmother, 'Flo, it's like being in a prison with all those bars on the window.' Little did they know that the social club was Colchester's refurbished lock hospital, a military prison previously used to incarcerate prostitutes. It was demolished a few years later and only its prison wall remains.

Contents

List of illustrations	viii
List of abbreviations	ix
Acknowledgements	xi
Introduction	1
1 Colchester's Victorian garrison	21
2 The life of the prostitute, cradle to grave	33
3 Hannah Murrells and Thomas Platford	53
4 Men who encouraged prostitution	62
5 The Lifeboat and The Anchor	84
6 The Contagious Diseases Acts and the lock hospital	95
7 Policing prostitution	110
8 The role of Colchester's solicitors	127
9 Adjudicating prostitution	140
10 The Ship at Headgate	160
11 Reformers and neighbours	168
Conclusion	188
Bibliography	197
Index	203

Illustrations

1	Colchester High Street, 1858	2
2	Portion of Thomas Dobson's letter to the *Essex Standard*, 11 December 1857	10
3	Colchester Camp *c.*1880	22
4	Map of Colchester	23
5	Colchester High Street *c.*1890	30
6	The Mermaid in Mersea Road	36
7	Maidenburgh Street	56
8	Platford's brothel reported in the Essex Standard (1859)	57
9	A portion of the 1881 census for Stanwell Street	60
10	The British Hotel, West Stockwell Street	72
11	The Colchester Arms, Magdalen Street	74
12	Advertisement for the Artillery Arms 1867	76
13	Map of Magdalen Street	86
14	Colchester's lock hospital plan	99
15	The lock hospital wall	99
16	Mr Edward Waylen, Colchester's first borough medical officer	100
17	'Marmalade' Emma and Teddy Grimes *c.*1910	118
18	Mr Henry Jones, solicitor	130
19	A view of Lexden	131
20	Dr Williams, borough magistrate	147
21	Headgate viewed from Crouch Street *c.*1906	163
22	Mrs Round's Refuge for Fallen Women, Ipswich Road	174
23	The orphanage at the junction of Brook Street and East Hill	176
24	Middle Mill on the Colne, near North Bridge	193

Abbreviations

BMJ	*British Medical Journal*
ERO	Essex Record Office
ES	*Essex Standard*
IJ	*Ipswich Journal*
SRO	Suffolk Record Office
TNA	The National Archives, Kew

It is not necessary to prove that there is this connexion between drunkenness and crime, as this is an admitted fact: wherever public-houses and beer-shops abound there vice and crime abound also. Here, then, is something which can be dealt with; and I hesitate not to say that if the moral character of Colchester is to be bettered the system of almost indiscriminate public-house licensing must be altered, and the character and doings of existing drink-selling places strictly looked into; and if we must have such places they must not be allowed to remain what many of them are—public-house, gambling-house, and brothel all in one; filthy sinks of iniquity and moral nuisances to the neighbourhood in which they stand.

I shall, perhaps, be excused for quoting from the report of the Chaplain of Kirkdale Gaol. He says, "Whilst our towns are allowed to remain in the demoralized state which I am called upon year after year to deplore, and the beer-houses and night-houses are gaping on all sides and at all hours for their victims; whilst music and other exciting amusements are diverted from their innocent and desirable purpose of cheering the vacant hours of the toil-worn mechanic, and made to pander to the vices and excesses of the haunts of immorality, in which our criminal population are bred and nurtured, the schoolmaster may open his doors and instruct in every street, the clergy may exhort and warn with all earnestness, the gaol chaplain may strain every nerve to reclaim and reform; but I feel convinced that the labours of all, if (which God forbid) they be not wholly fruitless, will at least be miserably crippled, and too often paid with bitter disappointment."

Some such ideas as these have, no doubt, presented themselves to the mind of our worthy Mayor; and I am, therefore, rejoiced to hear him so boldly express his determination to attempt the adoption of some measures, not only to prevent the further increase, but to drive back, the tide of vice and immorality which is sweeping through our town; and this, whether he is supported or not. But on this point he need not fear; he is sure to be supported by the sympathy of all those whose sympathy is worth having—those who have at heart the welfare of their fellow beings. I trust that he may meet with all the success he can wish for, and that our town may become as conspicuous for its moral as it is for physical beauty and cleanliness.

I remain, Sir, your obedient Servant,
St. John's Street, Nov. 30th, 1857.   THOS. DOBSON.

Figure 2. Portion of Thomas Dobson's letter to the *Essex Standard*, 11 December 1857, deploring the increase of immorality in Colchester. Very few men chose to have such views published. Occasionally the newspaper's editor wrote a piece in this vein.

Some men may have feared retribution such as ridicule or broken windows if they interfered or made complaints. If any felt uneasy at condoning such a trade, they hid it behind empty words and charitable gestures, at least until a national movement to reduce prostitution began to make progress in the 1880s.

Local history studies of prostitution feature throughout this book and were very helpful in our assessment of the elements of Colchester's story that were unique. They focus on nineteenth-century prostitution in localities such as Kent, York, Plymouth and Southampton.[20] This, however, is the first to study Colchester's vice trade in depth. Colchester is fortunate to have several fine histories, from Philip Morant's of 1748 and Thomas Cromwell's of 1825 to those produced by the Victoria County History, Geoffrey Martin, Arthur Brown and Andrew Phillips.[21] None of these has much, if anything, to say about women's contribution or significance to the life of the town. The University of Essex also has a collection of theses on various subjects to do with Victorian Colchester.[22] But few consider working-class women – or prostitution – or suggest the involvement of prostitution in social change in the town. The group of middle-class women in Colchester who sought to improve the lives of working-class girls and divert or rescue them from prostitution has also sunk into undeserved obscurity.

Why was it difficult to control prostitution?

In the first place, prostitution was not illegal. Provided sexual congress was in private between consenting adults over the age of consent, no crime was committed. The authorities encountered some intractable difficulties in their attempts to reduce the impact of prostitution and, in the absence of effective laws, they employed a variety of alternative approaches without much success. Then, under pressure from the army, parliament passed a series of Contagious Diseases Acts in the 1860s that were intended to identify and imprison prostitutes affected with venereal symptoms in garrison towns and ports. The army saw this as the only practical solution to the soaring numbers of soldiers hospitalised with venereal disease, but Christian moralists were repelled by the idea of subjecting women to intimate medical examinations and to returning healthy prostitutes back into society to continue what was judged to be their immoral and destructive way of life. To the moralists the CDAs represented state licensing of sinful practices and they orchestrated an energetic and successful political campaign which brought about the repeal of the acts in 1889. Only then did parliament pass an act that permitted the *police* to summon brothel keepers. Prior to this it had been the responsibility of the parish vestry – minister and churchwardens – to identify brothels, report them and pay the legal expenses for hearing the case. Most vestries, knowing that brothels sprang up and disappeared like mushrooms, preferred to spend their income on helping the deserving poor in their congregations.

aggression. The town's attorneys managed the town's legal business between them, so that only a few were involved in court cases that featured prostitutes and brothels. But most of them were property owners and some had additional business interests, including the ownership of beerhouses and tenements rented to prostitutes. The bench of magistrates were also businessmen or doctors who, if not involved in the trade, were responsible for issuing public house licences, some of which premises encouraged prostitution. Had it not been for the factual reporting of the local newspapers, such involvement in the vice trade by these members of society would not have been clearly visible. However, editorial comment on such subjects was uncommon, which suggests a general caution or lack of interest in exposing the vice trade to public view. The final chapter investigates how the ordinary citizens of Colchester, both poor and wealthy, neighbours and reformers, dealt with prostitution. Since prostitutes lived and worked in almost every parish they could be seen and heard by anyone who knew how to recognise them. Sometimes they attracted crowds of followers in the street. They were not invisible women. But for feminists, Quakers and others with a religious conscience, Colchester's prostitutes were a real challenge. We give examples of some brave women who were not afraid to associate with the town's 'unfortunates', to offer them an alternative to life on the streets and to raise the substantial funds needed to find a place in a reformatory for those wishing to make a new start. Others concentrated on girls and women they hoped to divert from prostitution altogether by spending many hours encouraging a sense of self-worth and morality through education and sociability that did not involve alcohol.

The primary sources
Much of the material for this book comes from local newspapers, particularly the *Essex Standard*, which was first issued on 7 January 1831. For its first nine months it was printed in Chelmsford, before being acquired by John Taylor and Henry Riddell of Colchester in August 1831. In 1850 it was relatively expensive, thanks to the Newspaper and Stamp Duties Act of 1819, and cost 5d for four pages of seven columns of information published weekly. From 1855, following the abolition of stamp duty, it was issued twice a week, its circulation rose and it began to include some journalistic input.[23] By 1900 it cost 1d for eight pages, the chief difference (apart from the price) being a slight increase in white space on the page, an advantage paid for by advertisers. The news continued to be tightly packed into columns, with news illustrations a rare addition.[24]

This was a conservative newspaper for a town that usually returned conservative MPs[25] and, as Andrew Phillips observed, its editor John Taylor, proprietor of the *Standard* for 35 years from 1831, 'showed a rare willingness to jeopardise his circulation (or to increase it) by his trenchantly-held beliefs'. For instance, as a direct result of Taylor's refusal to support Lord John Manners in the parliamentary election of 1852 a rival newspaper, the *Gazette*, was started up by Manners' supporters. Taylor was particularly critical of the misuse of public funds and the use of public office for personal advantage. These beliefs in the end finished his career when, in 1866, he published an anonymous letter in his newspaper which unwisely accused a committee of borough commissioners of profiting from their relationship with the town's gas company.[26] The *Standard* was then sold to Edward Benham, T. Ralling[27] and Henry Harrison. Benham and Harrison was a publishing, printing and bookselling business in the High Street. Benham died in 1869, leaving the business in the capable hands of his widow and sons and Harrison. His son William Gurney Benham trained as a reporter and, from 1884 until his death in 1944, managed the business and edited the *Standard*, incorporating *The Essex and West Suffolk Gazette* in 1873. Arthur Brown describes Benham as one of a group of prominent local industrialists who 'saw themselves as a progressive, yet enlightened influence in the town's modernization'.[28]

The role of the press changed during John Taylor's lifetime, as journalistic input developed from the 1850s. One feature of this change was that local newspapers became 'a platform from which the discontented could attack the authorities'. They also became a means of educating the middle class about the lives of the poor.[29] The *Standard* was not a neutral newspaper. Under Taylor's editorship it was a strong supporter of Anglican and Tory values. In comparison with the *Essex Telegraph* and the *Essex and West Suffolk Gazette*, for instance, it was restrained in its reporting of sensational material. For this reason we consulted local newspapers of a different political hue, such as the *Ipswich Journal*, *The Essex Newsman* and the *Essex Telegraph*, in order to search for stories not carried by the *Standard* and to check for alternative accounts of the same story. The newspapers' prolific reporting around the subjects that we were researching – such as petty crime, public house licensing and inquests – included, like every primary source used by historians, biases, deficiencies and inaccuracies, and this was another reason for cross-checking stories between newspapers. In addition, as Lee has pointed out, 'the routine reporting of local magistrates' court hearings has yet to be fully explored as a journalistic genre in its own right'.[30] It would be good to know a little more about how the reporter went about the task of writing up the court business. There is no doubt that the intention was to report accurately as, from time to time, objection was made through letters to the press that the facts had been recorded wrongly and, on each occasion, the editor or reporter replied to deny this. The editor exercised his role by reducing a long and unedifying discussion to its gist only, but it is unclear the extent to which the reporter also did this. Where prostitution or some brothel activity was the focus, while names, occupations and addresses were generally carefully recorded, more titillating details were often glossed over in the *Essex Standard*. While a description of the woman's appearance was usually not included, the sordid details of her living conditions were given if relevant to the charge. This suggests that the reporter was merely recording the police evidence as it was read out by the constable. But, at other times, he was at pains to record the off-the-cuff witty repartee of some of the solicitors in their interactions with witnesses and magistrates, suggesting that the newspaper's readership was deliberately being entertained.

We employed other primary sources in an effort to understand the genre and to fill some of the gaps. For instance, the newspapers reported on events in the borough courts but, when space was limited and the subject unedifying, only the basic details were given and names were sometimes misheard and incorrectly recorded. Not every case that came before the borough Sessions was reported by the newspapers. The Sessions books were not a full record either, as they did not cover the period 1878–94, and no Petty Sessions records survived for the borough. However, the newspaper reports of Union Board of Governor meetings were much more informative than the bland minutes of these meetings, which can be read on microfilm in the Essex Record Office. The watch committee reports dealing with the borough police and the medical officer reports to the town council were also consulted. Colchester's sources rarely commented on prostitutes' appearance and they did not portray prostitutes as outsiders unless they actually came from a distant town. Rather, they fixed her firmly within a particularly disreputable element of the working-class community attached to family, friends, soldiers and neighbourhood.

Another important primary source was the nineteenth-century census, available on various specialist family history internet sites and also on microfilm at Colchester Library. Having discovered some transcription omissions and mistakes on the internet sites we used the microfilm copies to correct these.[31] The census allowed us to discover some household and family details unavailable in any other source and in some cases to discover the origins of prostitutes who were not local women. In this way we were also led to some new avenues of research. We were able to study particular streets in Colchester as reported in successive censuses to identify some of the brothel keepers mentioned in the press and to achieve an understanding of the town's development after the arrival of the garrison in terms of population increase and distribution. The census also allowed us to discover some details of the lives of the men associated with prostitution and also the family circumstances of the middle-class individuals – men and women – dedicated to improving working-class morality. Clearly, like the newspapers, the census has its limitations, not least the difficulty of confidently identifying individuals with common names. This compromised a section of our database, as explained in Chapter 2.

Combining these various primary sources allowed us to build up a more nuanced view of some of the individuals displayed in the newspaper stories. We also studied nineteenth-century maps and photographs of the town and investigated on foot what still remains of our period of interest.[32] We discovered that a good deal of information that enriched our database was reported in the sources without any apparent connection to vice or prostitution. For example, a solicitor might claim that a public house landlord was innocent of any court summons for disorderly conduct on his premises and this might be accepted without challenge by contemporary police and magistrates who had not searched their memories or their files. Our database sometimes revealed such claims to be untrue. This economy with the truth was also in evidence in the nineteenth-century tendency to mention difficult subjects obliquely.

Fragments of this story remain in Colchester to this day. The garrison is still in business, albeit on a different site. The lock hospital boundary wall still stands, carefully maintained by the borough council but lacking any explanatory plaque. People unknowingly inhabit houses in the town that were used as brothels and some of the women and the brothel keepers featured in this book have descendants living in the area. The name of at least one of the solicitors who feature in this story is a going concern in Colchester. For those who may want to research their own house or family story we have carefully footnoted our sources and intend to put our database on the web in due course. We hope that this new story of Colchester's Victorian past will help to illuminate some of the intractable problems with which the town engaged during that period and also pay tribute to the courage of the women who tried in their own way to survive against the odds – and sometimes succeeded – outside the Union workhouse.

Notes

1. A. Light, *Common People: The History of an English Family* (London, 2014).
2. A. Phillips, *Ten Men and Colchester* (Chelmsford, 1985), p. 53.
3. C. Lee, *Policing Prostitution, 1856-1886: Deviance, Surveillance and Morality* (London, 2013).
4. The Municipal Corporations Act of 1835 ensured the new elected town councils appointed a watch committee responsible for policing in the borough.
5. A.F.J. Brown, *Colchester 1815-1914* (Chelmsford, 1980), p. 37.
6. The Bluecoat School had taught boys and girls since 1710, while the Grammar School was an opportunity for the sons of Anglican 'free burgesses' in the town to access elite education. Fourteen Sunday Schools were opened in 1786. There were three almshouses and several charities providing food and clothing to the poor.
7. Brown, *Colchester*, pp. 91–5.
8. C. Emsley, *The Great British Bobby: A History of British Policing from the Eighteenth Century to the Present* (London, 2009), p. 126.
9. H. Kim, 'Charitable Associations in Colchester, 1800–1870: A Study of a Middle-class World' (unpublished PhD thesis, University of Essex, 2004).

10 W. Acton, *Prostitution considered in its Moral, Social and Sanitary Aspect in London and other Large Cities and Garrison Towns*, 1st edn (London, 1858), pp. 42 and 44.
11 M.P. Morgan, 'William Acton and Medical Discourse in Mid-nineteenth-century Britain' (unpublished PhD thesis, University of Essex, 2011).
12 H. Mayhew, *London Labour and the London Poor*, vol. IV (London, 1861).
13 S.K. Kent, *Sex and Suffrage in Britain, 1860–1914* (Princeton, NJ, 1987); J. Phegley, *Courtship and Marriage in Victorian England* (Santa Barbara, CA, 2012).
14 J. Rendall, *Women in an Industrialising Society: England 1750–1880* (Oxford, 1990).
15 L. Davidoff and C. Hall, *Family Fortunes: Men and Women of the English Middle Class, 1780–1850* (London, 1987).
16 T. Fisher, *Prostitution and the Victorians* (Stroud, 1997); J.R. Walkowitz, *Prostitution and Victorian Society: Women, Class and the State* (Cambridge, 1980); P. Bartley, *Prostitution: Prevention and Reform in England 1860–1914* (London, 2000); Kent, *Sex and Suffrage*; G. Petrie, *A Singular Iniquity: The Campaigns of Josephine Butler* (London, 1971).
17 K. Chesney, *The Victorian Underworld* (London, 1970); Bartley, *Prostitution*.
18 Fisher, *Prostitution* and *Times Literary Supplement*, 10 October 1997.
19 M. Shapiro and D.M. Hughes, 'Decriminalized Prostitution in Rhode Island: Impunity for Violence and Exploitation' (Academia edu., 2015).
20 Walkowitz, *Prostitution*; Lee, *Policing Prostitution*; Frances Finnegan, *Poverty and Prostitution: A Study of Victorian Prostitutes in York* (Cambridge, 1979).
21 P. Morant, *The History and Antiquities of the most Ancient Town and Borough of Colchester* (London, 1748); T. Cromwell, *History and Description of the Ancient Town and Borough of Colchester in Essex* (London, 1825); S. Durgan, *Colchester, 1835–1992: An Extract from the Victoria History of the County of Essex*, vol. 9 (London, 1997); G.H. Martin, *The Story of Colchester from Roman Times to the Present Day* (Colchester, 1959); Brown, *Colchester*; Phillips, *Ten Men and Colchester*.
22 A.F.F.H. Robertson, 'The Army in Colchester and its Influence on the Social, Economic and Political Development of the Town, 1854–1914' (unpublished PhD thesis, University of Essex, 1992). Kim, 'Charitable Associations in Colchester'.
23 R. Sindall, *Street Violence in the Nineteenth Century: Media Panic or Real Danger?* (Leicester, 1990).
24 The Essex Record Office holds the microfilm of editions from 1831 to 1931 and most editions from 1831 to 1900 (four years are missing) have been digitised by the British Library and are available on the web. Originals are held in the collection of the Essex Society for Archaeology and History in the library of the University of Essex.
25 The Liberals won elections here in both seats in 1868, 1880 and 1895.
26 Phillips, *Ten Men and Colchester*, pp. 4 and 61–3.
27 Thomas Ralling was a reporter and sub-editor on the newspaper for 30 years but died in 1869 aged 44, his experience as part proprietor and publisher a short one. Two of his sons followed him in the business.
28 Brown, *Colchester*, p. 51.
29 Sindall, *Street Violence*, p. 31.
30 Lee, *Policing Prostitution*, p. 60.
31 We are grateful to the University of Essex history department, who funded a year's subscription to Find My Past.
32 We are indebted to various interest groups in Colchester who have set up websites of photographs such as: <http://www.camulos.com/>; a Facebook group, Colchester for old Farts and Fogies <https://www.facebook.com/groups/225676564266003/>; <http://www.bowcott.com/postcards.htm#garrison>; and <http://www.colchesterhistoricbuildingsforum.org.uk/drupal/>.

CHAPTER 1

Colchester's Victorian garrison

There is not much to be said about soldiers' women. They are simply low and cheap, often diseased, and as a class do infinite harm to the service.[1]

Colchester's Victorian garrison was started in 1856. This chapter considers its impact on the town, both positive and negative. The army had its own rules and regulations that were outside the town's jurisdiction. The soldiers were free to roam when off duty and to patronise the town's leisure outlets, and they also went quite far afield to neighbouring towns and villages. They caused problems of law and order as well as public decency when they stripped off to swim in the river or lay with a prostitute in a field. But because the garrison also provided economic opportunities the town's authorities were unwilling to be censorious and preferred to negotiate with the garrison, encouraging the CO to assist the town where possible to keep the costs of policing down. In addition, the garrison's officers provided sporting and cultural events and social activities which many in the town enjoyed.

Colchester was used to the presence of soldiers on its streets well before the Victorian garrison's personnel arrived in the town in 1856 because the Essex Militia assembled there every summer for training lasting about two months. In May 1853 a public meeting was called to discuss how to instruct and entertain the 800 militia who were about to arrive, and a committee was set up. The committee secretary, a Crouch Street schoolmaster named Samuel Bradnack, contributed some of his 'young gentlemen' pupils to instruct the militia in reading, writing and accounts. He may have regretted this as, two years later, he described the militia as 'the heathen of Essex ... their notions of religion are not much in advance of the South Sea islanders'. He claimed that fewer than

100 of them could read and write and he disapproved of their enjoyment of the 'ribaldry, obscenity and sensuality of the taproom'.[2] Subsequently the militia's annual training often took place in the new garrison.

The War Office owned two sites in Colchester. One was the Old Barrack Ground off Port Lane. This had been the site of the Napoleonic barracks and was leased as a smallholding and cricket ground once the barrack huts were cleared after 1815. The other site was the Ordnance Field between Military Road and Butt Road. Together these two sites comprised about 45 acres, which proved to be insufficient as the garrison expanded. The War Office subsequently bought several farms in the vicinity to supply training grounds. The garrison used the Old Barrack Ground for several specific purposes. One was as a space to erect tents to provide extra billets when the camp was full. For instance, tents here accommodated 2,000 German Legion soldiers returning from the Crimea in the summer of 1856. Another was as the site of the lock hospital, erected in 1869 as a result of the Contagious Diseases Acts (CDAs). This hospital imprisoned prostitutes thought to be suffering from venereal disease, as explained in Chapter 6. The field was also sometimes used for drill and sporting purposes.

The Ordnance Field was the site of the camp. Wooden barrack huts were built here sufficient to house 3,000 men. Although the huts were erected with double walls by Messrs Lucas of Ipswich it seems that they were intended as temporary structures. A letter printed 12 years later from a 'shivering soldier' complained that the huts were situated 'on the highest hill in Essex' and that they were already worn out, the wind whistling through them as if they were paper. Nevertheless, they remained in use for nearly 40 years, being eventually demolished in 1893.[3] Contemporary photographs show the huts separated by wide gravel walks and with a parade ground to one side. The new barracks was,

Figure 3. Colchester Camp from *The Queen's Album* (Rock & Co, c.1880).

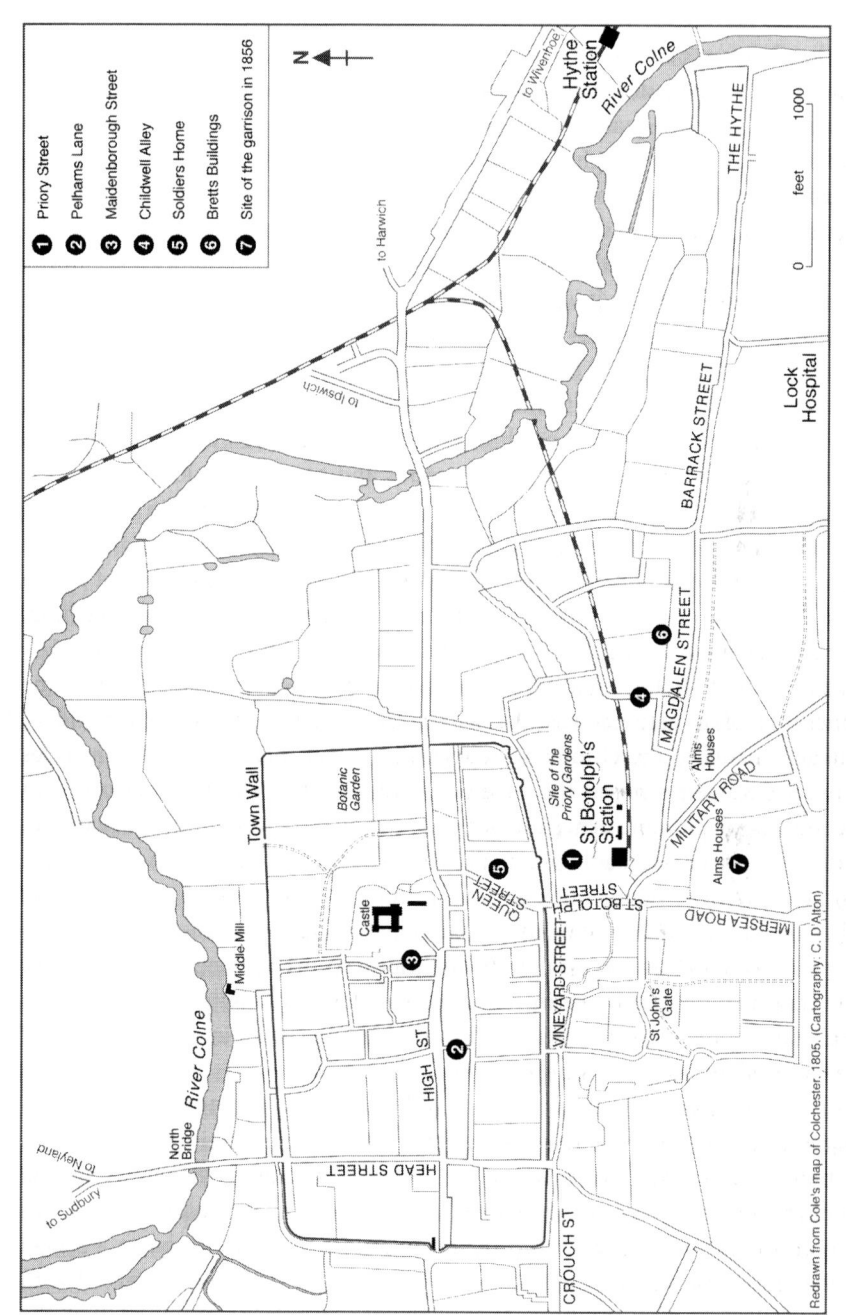

Figure 4. Map of Colchester showing the Roman walls, the site of the 1856 garrison and some of the streets associated with prostitution.

to India' and military schools. 'He should be very glad to think that the first petition on this subject came from the town of Colchester.'[39]

This meeting, held in public 11 years after the arrival of the garrison, was a classic example of how Victorian Colchester dealt with such social difficulties. Using the 'sanitary' euphemism, the mayor and his friends accepted the evidence that prostitution was causing an unacceptable rate of venereal disease and associated loss of manpower at the camp. They chose to lay the blame for this firmly at the door of a government that did not allow sufficient resources to educate and divert young soldiers from dissipation and drunkenness in their free time. Only one voice identified the local issue of the superfluity of beerhouse brothels in the town and this voice was ignored in the mayor's summing up. The complacency of the mayor in congratulating the town for raising the issue is noteworthy. It is hard to know whether he was saving the town from the likely effect on public order of closing down the worst beerhouses or whether he genuinely felt the 'sanitary' issue was for the army rather than the town to resolve. As we shall see in a later chapter, the *Standard*'s editor became increasingly critical of this laissez-faire attitude.

Conclusion

The arrival of the garrison encouraged a number of enterprises and vested interests to flourish, while controls to moderate the worst excesses took some time to develop and were imposed chiefly from outside in the shape of new legislation, as mentioned in the Introduction. The town's businesses that

Figure 5. Colchester High Street c.1890, several years before the present Town Hall was built.

provided coal, food, fodder, alcohol, clothing, laundry, boots and building services prospered, and competition for government contracts spread through the local area.[40] The garrison was the largest employer in town as well as a strong link to national affairs. It also employed civilians, both men and women, the latter as domestic servants, laundry workers and nursemaids. As the largest permanent building project the town had seen, its engineers stimulated the authorities to get to grips with sewage disposal, water and energy supply and highway improvements, including street lighting, although the finance to achieve these public works remained in short supply in Colchester. Private enterprise was a little more dynamic. Within a year of the soldiers' arrival 36 plate-glass windows had been installed in shops in the High Street and before long the determination to remove the market (and the inconvenient St Runwald's church) from this shopping street was clear. Property owners and borough officials were determined to bring the town into the modern era and to take advantage of the reviving economy. At regular intervals the town was enlivened (or disturbed) by the comings and goings of regiments, by royalty bent on inspection of troops and by rumours around the army's intentions for the development of the garrison. Some soldiers also contributed as individuals to the well-being of the town by acting heroically when the fire alarm sounded or when bathers got into difficulty in the river. And in the same decade that Robert Fitzroy began to publish his weather forecast in *The Times* the officer in charge of the camp's meteorological instruments began publishing his recordings in the *Standard*.[41]

But the arrival of the garrison also brought specific problems that were difficult to deal with. In addition to regular episodes of fighting and thieving, some soldiers demonstrated offensiveness and aggression on the streets in new and alarming ways. We give examples in Chapter 4 of some violent reactions on the part of local men whose girlfriends had left them to take up with soldiers. Chapter 2 shows how some parents were dismayed by their daughters' promiscuous behaviour with soldiers. From the start the garrison both contributed and drew attention to the insanitary living conditions endured by poor women and their families. It was responsible for the very large numbers of local women who were drawn into prostitution but, in the paternalistic culture of that period, its tendency was to blame them rather than the garrison for the ensuing venereal disease problem.

Notes

1   Mayhew, *London Labour*.
2   *ES* 2 November 1855.
3   *ES* 7 December 1855 and 15 January 1868.
4   *ES* 30 January 1856.
5   Soldiers' wives and children were not included in the army medical service until 1878.
6   A. Skelley, *The Victorian Army at Home: The Recruitment and Terms and Conditions of the British Regular, 1859–1899* (London, 1977), Chapter 1.

7   *ES* 30 March 1895.
8   Skelley, *The Victorian Army at Home*, pp. 26–7. In some years as many as 20 per cent of Colchester's inquests were into the deaths of soldiers, both serving and pensioned.
9   R. Pearsall, *Night's Black Angel: The Forms of Victorian Cruelty* (London, 1975), p. 195.
10 P. Cox, 'Compulsion, Voluntarism, and Venereal Disease: Governing Sexual Health in England after the Contagious Diseases Acts', *Journal of British Studies*, 46 (2007), pp. 91–115.
11 Army Medical Department Statistical, Sanitary and Medical Reports for the year 1862. Parliamentary Papers 1864 vol. XXXVI: 89, p. 12.
12 In 1888 the CO issued another ban on unaccompanied women entering the camp. *ES* 28 April 1888.
13 *ES* 22 October 1862.
14 This Society had commenced operations in 1844. *ES* 3 December 1856.
15 O. Anderson, 'The Growth of Christian Militarism in Mid-Victorian Britain', *The English Historical Review*, 86/338 (1971), pp. 46–72.
16 *ES* 23 February 1877.
17 *ES* 23 August 1879. The curate of St Martin's suggested that a similar reading room might be provided for the town's working men. *ES* 15 June 1889.
18 Robertson, 'The Army in Colchester', p. 67; M. Trustram, *Women of the Regiment: Marriage and the Victorian Army* (Cambridge, 1984). The 1881 census shows that Colchester Camp housed 257 wives and 363 children, making up nearly a quarter of the garrison. The percentage of married soldiers had more than doubled in twenty years.
19 TNA, WO 33/3.
20 The *Colchester Gazette* reported a married driver in the Royal Artillery punished for claiming to be unmarried when he enlisted. *Colchester Gazette* 5 December 1877.
21 *ES* 20 March 1857.
22 Trustram, *Women of the Regiment*, pp. 167–8.
23 *ES* 9 January 1857.
24 After a month the mother disappeared and the foster mother applied to the father for money to raise the little girl. *ES* 31 December 1881.
25 *ES* 12 January 1884.
26 *ES* 23 November 1860.
27 *ES* 26 November 1856.
28 *ES* 5 December 1856.
29 *ES* 3 December 1856.
30 *ES* 11 February 1868.
31 *ES* 4 December 1857.
32 Martin, *The Story of Colchester*, p. 103.
33 *ES* 14 August 1857.
34 The average number was anticipated to be 30 or 40 military prisoners at any one time – about 10 per cent of the prison's capacity.
35 *ES* 21 April 1858.
36 *ES* 31 December 1869.
37 *ES* 1 November 1865.
38 *ES* 25 June 1858. Pickets were soldiers tasked with policing off-duty soldiers.
39 The whole meeting is reported in *ES* 20 March 1867. The word 'petition' probably did not carry the modern meaning of a formal written request with many signatories.
40 A letter to the *Standard* complained that the initial coal contract had been given to an Ipswich firm without a prior advertisement. *ES* 18 January 1856.
41 *ES* 16 August 1867.

CHAPTER 2

The life of the prostitute, cradle to grave

*She had never been on the streets except
when she wanted things for the children.*[1]

If the police labelled a woman as 'prostitute' or 'unfortunate' when presenting her case in court it was as a result of some research into her behaviour, associates and activities. They were identifying a woman who had been apprehended for a crime such as theft, assault or drunken disorder and adding 'unfortunate' as an extra explanatory identifier in much the same way as they described male miscreants as 'carpenter' or 'publican'. They were conveying to the court the information that the woman derived her income from the vice trade. This assessment was almost never challenged in court. Nevertheless, it is hard to see Colchester's prostitutes as representing just another of the town's occupations, as their individual circumstances varied widely. For every full-time prostitute there were many others who also had a day job in a bar or a factory. Their ages ranged from 12 to 40 and most had grown up in ordinary working-class families. Some worked from brothels, others shared lodgings with another prostitute or lived alone. Most were unmarried but some had cohabitation arrangements and a number found husbands and ceased prostituting themselves. A few were encouraged back into prostitution by their husbands or by widowhood. Becoming a prostitute was not a one-way street and some found ways to leave prostitution without the help of moral reformers. What most of them had in common when they began was youth, poverty and a long, hard working day.

It seems likely that, once the garrison arrived in 1856, Colchester's prostitutes rapidly increased in number, although we also have to acknowledge the claim made by the Reverend Meshach Seaman in 1842 that there were in the town 'more than 400 unhappy females, some of whom do not exceed the age of 14 who are living partly or wholly upon the wages of sin'.[2] The mayor did not hold this opinion, confidently claiming in 1854 that the town had hitherto enjoyed a reputation 'for having fewer [women] of that class'.[3] Perhaps he was ignoring the part-time prostitutes in his count.

We have constructed a database of 337 women who are described in at least one Colchester source, in the period 1850–1900, as a prostitute, or by one of the several euphemisms used for that term, such as 'unfortunate', or who are named as lock hospital patients.[4] The sources of information include the records of the borough Sessions and the watch committee, local newspapers (including their inquest reports), census records, birth and marriage registrations and Board of Guardian minutes. The descriptions of the activities that brought the women before the court as defendants, complainants or witnesses quite often contain significant details about their way of life that can be followed up in other sources. Several years of intensive research have made us aware of the difficulties of tracking prostitutes in the records, however. Many kept a low profile, used aliases and married names or allowed reformers to give them new names. Reporters and minute-takers did not invariably record the names correctly or give ages and addresses.

The database has been sorted into three categories. For 40 (12 per cent) of the women it has been possible to collect a considerable amount of information about their families, their adult lives, where they lived, whether they married and had children, and when and where they died. One reason for the wealth of information was that these women, in contrast to the other groups in the database, made Colchester their home for a long period and often returned to the town even if marriage took them away. Many of them also misbehaved multiple times, coming to the attention of the authorities, their antics recorded by the newspaper. Thirteen of them died before their 30th birthday and 14 lived beyond the age of 59. Twenty secured husbands and nine had children with or without marriage. Five of them also experienced reformatories. This little group forms the core of the database, but the extent to which they represent the whole database is debatable.

Another 117 women (35 per cent of the database) are 'invisible' women who left hardly any trace in the primary sources. Some 78 per cent of this group feature just once, perhaps in a drunken escapade or listed as a patient in the lock hospital, and the details of their existence before and after this episode are unknown. The remaining 22 per cent of this 'invisible' group can be traced for no more than four years. Successful tracking clearly depends on names remaining the same through time and on the individual being alive and willing to record her existence on census night. This group's lack of any census record or birth registration *before* their apparent fall from grace is a puzzle, suggesting that they may have given false names to those in authority and that they were only able to do this convincingly because they were strangers in Colchester and subsequently left the town. If they resided in Colchester only for a matter of months, used a false name and left as soon as they fell foul of the law, resorting to another name thereafter, this might explain the dearth of information. Other prostitutes also used false names but the police usually referred to them by both their names, which suggests that some level of detective work was carried out. This group is also a reminder that accepting the definition of 'prostitute' used by those in authority is fraught with difficulty. Perhaps some of these 117 'invisible' women decided that enough was enough and managed, or were assisted, to resist vice after their first encounter with court or hospital. But why would they subsequently fail to be recorded in the census or in the marriage or burial records? Did they reform and change their name again or did they die unknown and friendless? Alternatively, a few may have moved abroad as camp followers and stayed or died abroad. Others may have been able to pay their way out of encounters with the police. Some nineteenth-century novelists presented the prostitute as a woman beyond the pale, an embarrassment to her family, an invisible creature of the night. This section of the database gives some credence to this view.

The remaining 180 women (53 per cent of the database) fall between these two contrasting groups. These women's years as prostitutes in Colchester are well recorded and it has been possible to find many of them in the census as children, but then, as in the 'invisible' group, the record fades. Some 54 per cent of this third group have been traced to the age of 39 and we have no knowledge of their lives after this age. A third were traced to the age of only 19. Some had common or local names, making identification difficult. Those who married a soldier and were posted abroad did not invariably return.

In short, for about two-thirds of the 337 women on the database we have a surprising amount of information and, for the rest, next to none. Lee's study of towns in Kent used a database of 500 women, 200 of whom could be linked between two or more sources.[5] Judith Walkowitz's case studies of Plymouth and Southampton prostitutes researched in the 1970s claim that 40 per cent of the women in these towns aged 15 to 29 were prostitutes.[6] We would not feel confident claiming such a high figure for Colchester. The relevant censuses record 10,000–12,000 females in the town, a little over 3,000 of whom were in the age group selected by Walkowitz.

Whether or not we accept Reverend Scaman's numbers (quoted above), he was correct to note that some prostitutes were very young. Some 19 per cent of the core database was aged 12 to 16 when first apprehended. At this point the age of consent, which was 12, was linked to the age at which girls could expect to be earning their own keep rather than to any considerations of morality. In other words, a girl old enough to be earning for herself was considered to be old enough to make her own decisions. Moral considerations came into focus in 1885 when the age of consent was raised to 16.

Figure 6. The Mermaid in Mersea Road, 'the pest of the neighbourhood', where Maria Grant was introduced to soldiers and became a 'bad character'.

Some of those who worked in a brothel or a beerhouse had adult encouragement in the form of a mother figure. Maria Grant, aged 12, was persuaded by the Mermaid's landlady to work there. She told the magistrate 'she considered she was to go there as a servant, but on arrival there she was introduced to soldiers, and had since become a bad character'.[7] Ann Johnson, distressed when her soldier sweetheart left town without her, was encouraged by the landlady of the Gardener's Arms, where she began to work as a prostitute – a letter from a friend quoted at her inquest said of the landlady 'she has done so much for you, and more than your own mother'.[8] Ellen Jones, arriving destitute from Winchester, perhaps a camp follower, fetched up at the Yorkshire Grey in 1857, where landlady Mrs Popps 'very kindly took her into her house and gave her lodging and food'.[9] Subsequently Ellen was a lock hospital patient. Others may have been following the example of a workmate or fellow lodger or have been rebelling against parental rules. Sarah Ann Woodford's mother said she had 'been leading a very irregular life; she got into bad company',[10] while Susannah Taylor's mother refused point blank to take her back. 'She had taken her home seven times, and tried to save her from her present life, but she had returned.'[11]

A small number had spent a significant time in a workhouse or orphanage as children, and others, of course, may have spent shorter periods there, but the database suggests that the institution was rarely a direct introduction to life on the streets. One exception was Hannah Murrells, who went to Stanway Union with two of her siblings when her father died. She was rebellious as an inmate and accused of immodest behaviour in chapel, and within months of quitting the institution had begun cohabiting with a local brothel keeper (see Chapter 3). Another exception was Cartata Deal, sent on her father's death when she was 13 from Colchester to the Soldiers' Daughters' Home in Hampstead. She returned to Colchester in her mid-teens, became a prostitute and died in her twenties. But the majority of those we have traced lived their childhood in a family setting and many in the core database died having experienced a family setting in their mature years. The Union workhouse remained a factor in their lives: a place many tried to avoid, a place where some mothers deposited their children while continuing to work as prostitutes from lodgings or brothel. For some prostitutes the workhouse foul ward was a refuge from unemployment when suffering a bout of venereal disease.

Most daughters of working parents were encouraged to start work that would support their own living costs some time around their 12th birthday. Emma Griffin's claim that the average age for children starting work was ten and, for children in industrial towns, seven is not upheld in Colchester's sources.[12] Apart from a few small girls who acted as nursemaids to the children of working mothers, we have scant evidence of girls younger than 12 employed in commercial settings in Colchester. The age at which a girl began work depended to some extent on the economic status of the parents, the girl's position in the family, her usefulness as a female at home supporting the other workers in the household and her own desire for independence.[13] Some of those beginning work at this young age continued to live at home with their parent(s) and siblings while working in a local shop or clothing factory, as outworkers, as nursemaids and laundresses on the garrison, or even as prostitutes. Others left home as teenagers, took lodgings, a room alone or shared, or lived with their employer's family. Some employers took advantage of their vulnerability and a few girls brought complaints of indecent assault and rape to court. It was usually impossible for the girl to find a witness to her resistance, while medical evidence was generally inconclusive because it was sought too late after the indecent act. One exception was the case brought against Thomas Folkard, landlord of the Flying Fox, Harwich Road, who was charged with raping his 13-year-old servant. The case was serious enough to be referred by the borough Sessions to the next Assize, where he received a sentence of nine months' hard labour.[14]

Colchester's silk-spinning factories employed large numbers of teenage girls working long hours for small wages. Had the wage been steady it might have been easier for the women to pay their way, but such records as we have of women's wages in local factories suggest that the wage varied week on week owing to vagaries in trade, machine breakdown and illness. Tailoring and dressmaking also brought in erratic wages. In a letter printed in the *Essex Standard* in 1846 it was claimed that

> with the utmost industry a bare maintenance can scarcely be procured [since] the price for making a pair of trousers for a boy is only 5d, out of which the women find their own thread; for a man only 6d and for *best* trousers 10d, finding their own silk twist.[15]

This remained the situation in 1892, when a meeting was held in Colchester to rally support for a women's union. The meeting was chaired by the rector of All Saints, who said 'the state of things as regarded women's wages in Colchester was a disgrace to every man'. When he asked his audience how much a woman could earn working ten hours a day at tailoring there was dead silence, broken only by a young man saying he would get the sack if he answered.[16]

In the introduction to her book *Adapting to Capitalism* Pamela Sharpe argues that capitalism increasingly marginalised women's work, reducing women's work opportunities and their earnings in relation to men's. Three issues in particular affected their access to work – low wages, ideological factors and a legal system that favoured men in relation to property ownership. She suggests that opportunities for women's work were reducing in the period before the garrison arrived in 1856 as a result of the loss of the wool-weaving trade and changes in agriculture, and emphasises women's poor remuneration in comparison with men, arguing that this was an explanation both for women marrying at an earlier age than their mothers and for the increasing problem of female vagrancy in Essex. There is evidence to show that women's wages in this part of Essex were depressed for much of the nineteenth century. Sharpe claims that, *early* in the nineteenth century, female weavers at Courtauld's silk mill at Halstead earned 10s or more per week.[17] However, the paybook for Courtauld's Panfield Lane silk factory in Braintree in 1827 shows that by that date nobody was receiving so much. Even the overseers had only 8s a week. A sample of the 100 female factory hands shows that 5s was an exceptional wage and also that wages varied considerably week on week, from nothing (presumably when the woman was ill or caring for a family member) to the occasional 6s a week.[18] Judy Lown's study of Courtauld's business confirms that in 1861 average earnings for most of Courtauld's female workers were no more than 8s a week. The children who were too young to weave (less than 17 years of age) earned 2s–4s 6d a week.[19] Arthur Brown said of Colchester that the girls in the St Peter's Street silk mill earned about 5s for a 70- to 80-hour week, adding that this remuneration was in real terms less than 'the 3s to 4s received by their grandmothers at woollen-spinning in the previous century'.[20] The girls who worked for Hyam's tailoring business in Colchester probably earned not much above 1s a day. In Mayhew's view such women were 'toiling so long and gaining so little, and starving so silently and heroically, round about our very homes'.[21]

These fabric and clothing businesses were all susceptible to periods of boom and bust, which affected their workers' ability to budget, to enjoy the fruits of their labour and to save for marriage. For a 12-year-old child starting work the wages were insufficient to allow her to be confidently independent. It was not possible to find adequate lodgings, food and clothing on 2s a week. These girls either continued to live at home, no doubt giving all their earnings to a parent, or lodged with a family member for a short period. The census enumerator sometimes even described such youngsters as 'lodgers' in their own parental households. There were many make-do-and-mend resolutions to the problems arising from erratic and low wages. One of the functions of the pawn shop for its customers was to help smooth over short-term cash-flow problems and some women pawned their landlady's property on a regular basis. Provided the landlady did not notice her property had been borrowed in this way all was well. If she noticed and objected the woman risked being arrested for theft.[22] It was also possible to use the pawnshop to raise a loan on stolen property. In this case the customer had to have a convincing story ready to allay the pawnshop keeper's suspicions. So, in order to survive, some on the database resorted to theft, lived on short rations and supplemented their irregular income through prostitution, which, in a newly garrisoned town such as Colchester, was an increasingly available solution. It seems that many women kept their day job while supplementing their income in this way. For census purposes they described themselves as 'dressmaker' or 'silk factory hand', while for the full-time prostitutes the enumerator usually left that space on the form blank and only occasionally wrote 'prostitute'.

So the economic reasons for prostitution were understandable. A low rate of female wages coupled with work that could be erratic made it very difficult for young women to support themselves without some help from their family. Girls that followed the soldiers to Colchester left family support behind and became exposed to the difficulties of finding work and lodgings in an overcrowded town where they might be preyed upon by unscrupulous adults. Colchester's low-paid work was generally very hard, involving long hours and demanding employers. It took health and courage to withstand such demands and these qualities were difficult to maintain on low wages. Once women had crossed the threshold into full-time prostitution it may have seemed like a land of opportunity for some – the opportunity to enjoy the apparent freedom from a long working day and from hunger and oppression. Prostitutes went to beer shops and public houses to pick up customers and these were convivial places for some hours of the day. But, as we will see, it was also a potentially dangerous lifestyle choice and involved activities that earned for some of them public disgrace, imprisonment and venereal disease. Some began and ended their career as vagrants and some died as prostitutes. The average age at death for the core group on the database was 47 years but, of these, five died as teenagers and eight died in their twenties.[23] Several of these deaths involved inquests, either because the death occurred in a brothel and incurred neighbourhood suspicions that were relayed to the coroner or because the death was sudden or, in Ann Johnson's case, a suicide.

The demeanour of the women in public was often reported to have been noisy and rude, especially when they had been drinking. Under duress they swore, kicked and shrieked. In court their behaviour was related to their age and experience. A few resorted to tears – 'appeared much affected', as reported by the newspaper – or 'assumed an air of injured innocence'[24] or impudence, all of which may have been calculated behaviour. But many more expressed defiance and resentment. Elizabeth Hewitt, 'with an oath, declared that when she got her liberty she would break the old [complainant's] windows for giving her in charge'. Victoria Harmer shouted across the court at her accuser 'I hope God will punish you.' Annie Woods exclaimed 'One month! I will stand on my head and do it; and I will get drunk again when I come out. I don't care for you.' Ellen Moss, in court for riotous behaviour, received some advice from the mayor. He said, 'I wish something more could be done for you that might induce you to mend your ways.' Her response was 'Thank you sir. I hope you may sit there until I come out.' The mayor added another week to her sentence for this lack of respect.[25] Some cracked jokes in court or made ribald comments that caused laughter. The police sometimes claimed to be embarrassed by the women's language when they were arrested and passed notes to the bench rather than repeat the expletives in court. But defiance was not a wise strategy in the paternalistic setting of the borough court and it was usually employed as a last resort after sentencing, to redress a perceived injustice or loss of power. The women often lived a double life, working from lodgings by day and in the beerhouse after dark, trying to keep the two sites as separate spheres. Being arrested and examined in court disrupted this double life, which probably explains any last ditch defiance from the dock. Their shouting in court, in a state of sobriety, also made clear that they did not accept the role of deferential female and, like some suffragettes, they chose to confront paternalistic attitudes head on by shouting, assaulting policemen and smashing windows.

Some unruly groups in Colchester – such as soldiers or hooligan boys – were referred to as such by the *Essex Standard*, as they misbehaved collectively and were observed with alarm by the law-abiding. Colchester's prostitutes do not seem to have been a recognisable *group* in the town in this way. Occasionally the police or the local community complained about gangs of vagrant girls. Jane Lott, for instance, was part of a gang who 'got into all sorts of out of the way places to sleep, ... robbed gardens and other places, and behaved in a most disgusting manner'.[26] Judging from the details of the many theft cases in which they were involved, prostitutes as individuals seem not to have been easily spotted either on the pavement or in the shops or pawnshop when masquerading as customers. Mrs Whiting came to Colchester from Elmstead on a shopping expedition. She sheltered from the rain in a shop doorway in the High Street and was soon joined by two young women whom she judged to be 'respectable persons'. Two minutes later one of them stole Mrs Whiting's purse from her pocket and they turned out to be anything but respectable once the police began investigations.[27] Pickpocket and shoplifter prostitutes were able to fit into the scene as innocent participants, at least until the constable arrived. When Josephine Butler came to Colchester to support repeal of the Contagious Diseases Acts she described in a letter to her children how she dressed to be inconspicuous. 'I had not bonnet or gloves – only an old shawl over my head – and looked quite a poor woman.'[28] This is exactly how most of Colchester's prostitutes dressed. Many other poor women not labelled as 'unfortunates' committed similar petty crimes and anti-social activities in much the same places chosen by the prostitutes. So, much as the middle classes might have wished to avoid the town's 'fallen' women, this was difficult to achieve, as one poor woman looked much like another and, as the police found, considerable research had to be done to identify a prostitute or a brothel with confidence. It seems counter-intuitive to present Colchester's prostitutes as employing the camouflage of their class. Surely they had to be visible in order to attract their customers? Yet it was rare for the newspaper reports to describe a prostitute's appearance as in any way striking and arrests for street soliciting were very rare indeed, as most prostitutes plied their trade in the shelter of the beerhouse.

There were many different living arrangements available to Colchester's prostitutes and those who chose to remain in the town used different arrangements at different times. In some premises the girls were 'harboured' and managed by a man, woman or couple who lived on the premises.[29] Elsewhere the brothel was a freelance operation where one prostitute, often posing as a married woman, made herself responsible for the house rent while subletting individual rooms to other prostitutes. Many of the women running brothels were – or said they were – married and landlords usually claimed that they were renting the premises to a respectable married woman or that to live with her mother.⁵⁵ Georgina Went was another prostitute whose family support was crucial. Census records show that she lived with her mother, sisters, their children and two of her own, not leaving home until the death of her mother, when Georgina was in her forties. She then found a home in Brook Street that she shared for the next 30 years with some of her children and grandchildren.

Those without families had to find alternative child support if they were to keep their children with them rather than resorting to the Union's care. Nellie York, who agreed to spend time in a reformatory in Greenwich rather than be imprisoned for theft, came back to Colchester working as a kitchen maid in one of the High Street hotels. She had two children who are recorded living with her at Ipswich in 1891, where she had a job as a housekeeper. The children were toddlers while she worked in Colchester and, like many another poor woman in the town, she probably paid a neighbour or a child to care for them while she was at work.⁵⁶ Other single mothers, particularly towards the end of the nineteenth century, after the arrival of the NSPCC in Colchester, were identified as poor and neglectful mothers. Alice Dines did not manage to keep her two little boys. She was born in Frating, where she was recorded living with her parents and siblings in the 1871 and 1881 censuses. In the 1891 census they had all moved to Colchester and Alice's two illegitimate sons had joined the family. A year later Alice and her children were living in Magdalen Street in considerable poverty, where she was reported by the NSPCC for child neglect.⁵⁷ Alice 'had no other occupation excepting that of prostitute'; her children were discovered to be dirty and hungry and were taken to the Union to be fed while their clothes were fumigated. Alice denied she had been cruel to the children but was sentenced to a month's hard labour. Subsequently she married a soldier and managed to reclaim her boys. But, at the age of 34, the 1901 census shows the widowed Alice a prisoner in Ipswich jail, her two little boys back in the Union workhouse.⁵⁸

Census evidence demonstrates that some of the women on the database eventually married and had legitimate children who lived to be adult. Others managed to secure a husband even if motherhood was denied them. Edith Churchyard had an illegitimate child when she was 20 who survived less than eight months, being 'sickly from its birth'. She then began cohabiting with a private in the Norfolk regiment before moving to a brothel in North Hill. Some years later, when she was 31, she married the soldier she had lived with. When he died two years later she quickly remarried. The 1911 census reveals her living with her second husband and her widowed father but without children. Her death was registered in Colchester in 1941.

Even if marriage took the women away from Colchester they often returned. Prostitute Emily Fitch was 18 when she married a coach smith and moved with him to London. There were no children. When widowed she returned to the Hythe and supported herself as a tailoress, dying there in 1894 aged 51. Susannah Sach plunged into vagrancy and prostitution on the death of her parents. After a period in a reformatory she found herself in Stoke Newington, working as a cook. But she evidently kept contact with her birthplace, Tollesbury, and married a Tollesbury widower with two children when in her forties. Others remained where they were when widowed, finding new ways of supporting themselves as they always had. Jane Leech's husband took her to London where, after 15 years of childless marriage, she is recorded in Tottenham working as a midwife. Hannah Garland married at 22; her marriage was childless and, when widowed, she lived in Childwell Alley with two male lodgers, dying in 1913 aged 70. Emma Hines' story was very similar. She spent time in the lock hospital and married five years later at 22; her marriage was childless and lasted 20 years. When widowed she lived alone in Butt Road as a tailoress. Some marriages evidently came to grief. Amelia Norfolk married James Doyle in 1871 but in successive censuses she is recorded living alone in Stoke Newington, her husband absent on census night, keeping a coffee house in Camberwell, then living on her own means at Greenwich.

Conclusion
This sample of wives and mothers gathered from the database of 337 women suggests a number of ideas. The earlier the prostitute married the more likely she was to conceive children. Most of the childless prostitutes delayed marriage into their late twenties and beyond. Some moved into housekeeper–wife roles around their fortieth birthday. Their apparently low fertility was probably directly related to their unhealthy living conditions and the effects of sexually transmitted infections rather than to infanticide in its various forms. The low numbers of offspring meant that, when elderly or infirm, the women had to be self-reliant or depend on the Union. We expected to find some of them ending their days in the workhouse, as Hannah Murrells did. However, we have not found many, perhaps because of limitations in the census returns. Women who worked as prostitutes after 1865 would mostly have been able to avoid becoming workhouse inmates until after 1911, which is the last census currently available to view. Once the 1921 census becomes available we may be able to find some of the database names listed as workhouse inmates aged 60 or more. Once they were too old for prostitution, or married, these women become indistinguishable from other poor women and wives. This reformation, due to ageing, was meaningful and in most cases successful. It was possible for some to regain the status they had lost when they stood in the magistrates' court accused of misdemeanours by their social betters. Sometimes, indeed, they returned to court as respectable witnesses to neighbourhood disagreements. It

was possible to maintain supportive contact with their families. It was possible to return to their roots after time away.

Above all, Colchester's prostitutes were drawn from working-class communities. As children they witnessed their parents' struggle to feed and clothe the family on meagre wages and they had little access to education that might have given them better work opportunities. Prostitution was a young woman's game and for some it ended in marriage. Prostitutes who failed to marry or whose marriages ended through death or desertion by their husband had to find an alternative way of supporting themselves once they reached their forties. The 1911 census shows Emma Urkmacher, aged 46, working as a servant in a lodging house and Caroline Day, aged 70, a charwoman living with her two adult children. Both of these women are on the prostitute database. Others, such as Hannah Murrells, were forced into the workhouse when unable to work or to rely on support from their children. As we will see in Chapter 11, there were some middle-class initiatives in the town to divert girls from prostitution, just as there were initiatives in the garrison to divert soldiers from the beerhouse. But not every woman survived her prostitute years and lived into her fifties. Some died of syphilis, others of illnesses related to poverty and poor living conditions and a few chose to end an unbearable life through suicide.

Notes

1. The evidence of Mary Dicker who 'first went on the streets at her husband's request'. *ES* 29 December 1894.
2. *ES* 4 March 1842.
3. *ES* 26 July 1854.
4. The database also includes information on men who encouraged prostitution in a variety of ways, as described in Chapter 4.
5. Lee, *Policing Prostitution*.
6. Walkowitz, *Prostitution and Victorian Society*.
7. *ES* 15 May 1868.
8. *ES* 18 September 1867. Ann Johnson's story is related in detail in the final chapter.
9. *ES* 25 November 1857.
10. *ES* 18 October 1867.
11. *ES* 23 June 1876.
12. Colchester had several silk spinning factories employing largely women, but they did not compare in scale to the premises identified in Griffin's research. E. Griffin, *Liberty's Dawn: A People's History of the Industrial Revolution* (New Haven, CT, 2013).
13. In 1893 the minimum school-leaving age was raised from 10 to 11.
14. *ES* 6 November 1861.
15. *ES* 13 February 1846.
16. *ES* 16 January 1892.
17. P. Sharpe, *Adapting to Capitalism: Working Women in the English Economy, 1700–1850* (Basingstoke, 1996).

18 ERO, D/F 3/2/18.
19 J. Lown, *Women and Industrialisation: Gender at Work in Nineteenth-century England* (Cambridge, 1990).
20 Brown, *Colchester*, p. 128.
21 Rendall, *Women in an Industrialising Society*, p. 69.
22 L. MacKay, 'Why They Stole: Women in the Old Bailey 1779–1789', *Journal of Social History*, 32/3 (1999), pp. 623–39.
23 This was calculated from the age at death of 40 women.
24 Caroline Ham reported in *ES* 19 August 1857.
25 *IJ* 29 August 1868.
26 *ES* 23 August 1890. The observations were made by the head constable.
27 *ES* 7 October 1853.
28 J.E. Butler, *Personal Reminiscences of a Great Crusade* (London, 1911), p. 30.
29 'Harboured' women paid rent. Some landlords got around this by charging the girl per customer instead of rent. Lee, *Policing Prostitution*, p. 43.
30 *ES* 7 October 1853.
31 *ES* 21 July 1858.
32 *ES* 6 April 1895 and *ES* 28 November 1896.
33 *ES* 7 Feb 1889.
34 The following year prostitute Edith Churchyard was attacked in the same yard.
35 Fisher, *Prostitution*, p. 91.
36 A beerhouse was only allowed to sell beer, whereas a public house could also sell spirits. Licences for both premises were issued annually by the magistrates after 1869. Prior to this date beerhouses were licensed by the excise authorities.
37 *IJ* 22 September 1855.
38 *ES* 11 and 18 October 1884.
39 *ES* 25 September 1886.
40 J.R. Gillis, *For Better, for Worse: British Marriages, 1600 to the Present* (Oxford, 1985), p. 114.
41 *IJ* 13 June 1871.
42 *ES* 24 December 1856.
43 *ES* 5 April 1872. Alice's husband was a soldier serving in India.
44 Trustram debates this issue in chapter 8 of *Women of the Regiment*, arguing that the War Office did not accept responsibility for supporting the wives and widows of soldiers until the 1890s.
45 Phegley, *Courtship and Marriage*. Joanna Phoenix makes the same point for modern prostitutes who experience the paradox that their survival strategy is undermined by the relationships involved in survival: J. Phoenix, *Making Sense of Prostitution* (Basingstoke, 1999).
46 *ES* 29 December 1894.
47 *IJ* 13 June 1871.
48 Walkowitz, *Prostitution*, p. 17.
49 *ES* 6 April 1895.
50 *ES* 15 April 1864.
51 *ES* 19 October 1864.
52 *ES* 5 March 1892.
53 Most of the mothers accused of 'child murder' were women who were not prostitutes but employed in live-in domestic service. The birth took place in private and the baby was discarded in the privy or in a box under the bed, where it was soon detected.
54 *ES* 14 January 1893.
55 The 1851 and 1861 censuses recorded her living at the Hythe with her mother.

56 In January 1861 the *Essex Standard* reported the inquest into the death of an eight-year-old shoemaker's daughter named Sarah Willis. Sarah had been left in charge of a neighbour's three younger illegitimate children in a court off West Stockwell Street 'in their mother's absence'. In a prank that went wrong, Sarah and one of her charges were set on fire and Sarah died later that evening in the hospital.
57 The National Society for the Prevention of Cruelty to Children was founded in 1884 and arrived in Colchester by the early 1890s.
58 One of her sons is named on the Great Bentley war memorial.

CHAPTER 3

Hannah Murrells and Thomas Platford

AN ORDER OF EJECTMENT
Mr HW Jones appeared on behalf of the
Colchester Brewing Company Limited for
an order to eject Mrs Platford, a tenant
of the Company's in Stanwell Street.[1]

This chapter is a case study of one of Colchester's prostitutes, whose life in the town is recorded from cradle to grave in a variety of sources. It shows that, for some of the town's prostitutes, it was possible to live a long and successful life within the constraints of class and gender. Like many of the town's prostitutes at this date Hannah Murrells was drawn into prostitution as a teenager and was involved in brothel life for many years. But she was also unusual in a number of ways – her loyalty to her pimp Thomas over a period of nearly 30 years and her ability to have children and to be in a position to care for them, a responsibility which was beyond the capability of most prostitutes. She was also unusual in that the Union workhouse played an important part in her story, both as a child and as an old woman.

Hannah was born at Fordham Heath near Colchester in the summer of 1834.[2] Thirty years later the observation was made of Fordham Heath that, 'taking a circuit of two miles, there are 100 or more children without a Sabbath School instruction. We are too far from the village school for these children to attend.'[3] When the 1841 census was compiled there were five children living in farm worker Daniel Murrells' family – three siblings older than the six-year-old Hannah, and Henry, her baby brother, who was just ten weeks old. After Hannah's father died in 1842, aged 41, the family broke up and the three youngest children, Sarah, Hannah and Henry, were sent to the Lexden Union workhouse at Stanway for the remainder of their childhood. So whatever formal education Hannah received would have been delivered in the Union workhouse schoolroom. This was evidently not a good experience for any of the children. Henry died aged 13 and his older sisters both rebelled against the workhouse system in spectacular fashion by behaving immodestly at the compulsory Sunday worship, for which misbehaviour they were arrested.

> It appears from the statement of the governor that on the previous Sunday each of the prisoners went to the Union chapel with their faces painted, and upon being remonstrated with they assaulted himself and the porter, besides other disorderly conduct. Each of the prisoners was sentenced to fourteen days' hard labour in the county house of correction.[4]

Hannah was 14 when she exchanged the discipline of the workhouse for that of the house of correction at Chelmsford. This experience evidently did not chasten her and on her return she took to absconding from the Union and behaving in challenging ways that the authorities could not ignore. It is of course possible that, in Terri Apter's words, these pauper girls were actively choosing to find their own way of discovering 'the interplay between gender, culture and human possibility' outside the workhouse walls.[5] Alternatively, there may have been something specific about that particular workhouse to which they were objecting or reacting. Local Board of Guardian minutes reveal occasional accusations of sexual predation and bullying in Union workhouses, although at this date authority certainly did not see these girls as victims. And in this part of Essex there were, as yet, no charitable initiatives set up to rescue such females.[6] Hannah's extended family did not rescue her either.

In 1849, aged 15, Hannah and her sister, with another girl, all 'of bad character' and Union absconders, were charged with vagrancy, having been found sleeping rough in Copford. A local farmer, John Ambrose, brought the prosecution, claiming the girls had damaged his bean field.

> He also understood that they had been in the habit of collecting a number of idle boys and men together in the evenings, and were a complete nuisance in the parish. Under these circumstances he authorized the police to take them into custody the first time he caught them on his premises. – The Chairman told the prisoners that the Bench considered them very incorrigible and abandoned characters, and … they would be sentenced to the full punishment allowed by the law – viz three months' imprisonment with hard labour.[7]

Unless a woman was caught acting indecently in a public place she could not be charged with prostitution so Hannah was accused of vagrancy, even though she was technically a workhouse inmate. The workhouse system had lost control of her and had failed to transform her into a dutiful and honest servant. In addition, there was a vagrant gang element about the absconding girls which the authorities probably feared would be infectious if not stopped and which made it more difficult than usual to find jobs for these young women outside the workhouse. Farmer Ambrose's view was that Hannah and her friends were deliberately leading workmen astray – 'collecting' them together, encouraging their idleness and occasioning destruction of his property. He used the word 'nuisance', which carried a legal meaning akin to trespass as well as the workaday sense of annoyance and inconvenience. Lest he should be judged petty for bringing workhouse orphans before the bench, Mr Ambrose claimed to speak for his neighbours and to be protecting the whole parish, not just his own bean fields, from incorrigible girls. This idea was endorsed by the magistrates, who decided to give the harshest punishment they could. The girls were judged as they presented themselves, defiant, shameless and dangerous, having made victims of men and boys, and Hannah spent the rest of the year in prison. At the age of 15 her life as a prostitute was about to begin. The workhouse had taught her to sew and perhaps to read but she had rebelled against the Union ideal of discipline and submission to authority and had escaped, confident of her ability to live on her wits (judging by her later history). She soon fell in with a local man called Thomas Platford, with whom she lived for the rest of his life.

Thomas Platford was born in 1821 in Colchester, so was 13 years older than Hannah. At the age of 20 (when Hannah was beginning her life in the workhouse) he was living in Hog Lane[8] in Colchester with a tailoress, also 20, called Betsey Pearsons. The 1841 census describes him as a labourer and the local newspaper as a 'notorious character' because, during the 1840s, while Hannah was rebelling in the workhouse, Thomas came before the Colchester bench on several occasions for theft, violent assault of two women and two breaches of the peace in Black Boy Lane, Colchester.[9] Perhaps he met Hannah in one of Colchester's many beerhouses soon after she left jail around Christmas 1849 and made her a proposition which she did not refuse.

In 1851 Thomas and Hannah were living together in Ipswich.[10] She was a dressmaker and he was a labourer, but the census enumerator did not specify her exact relationship to Thomas; Thomas was the household head but Hannah was described as neither his wife nor his lodger. The appropriate space to describe her status was simply left blank. Since, soon afterwards, Hannah and Thomas would be living together in a Colchester brothel the likelihood is that, in Ipswich, they were supported by her earnings as a dressmaker/prostitute and his as a casual worker and petty dealer. After some months in Ipswich, Thomas Platford and Hannah Murrells returned to Colchester. They settled into a rented house on the west side of Maidenburgh Street, described by its owner as 'well-built and roomy … with a yard in the rear', which they ran as a brothel accommodating other prostitutes.[11]

Figure 7. Maidenburgh Street, where Thomas Platford ran his brothel.

Hannah Murrells soon learnt to prey on her customers and to make the most of the opportunities that came her way to rifle their pockets, knowing or hoping that most men would be too embarrassed to make a formal complaint and that Thomas Platford might protect her against an aggrieved customer. One of her victims, William Brooks, was not embarrassed. He was a wheelwright from Chappel who, on 8 January 1853, caught the train to Colchester to transact some business. Missing his train home to his wife and daughters, he returned to the town, where

> having been drinking somewhat freely, he was accosted by the female prisoner, with whom he went home, and in the course of the night examined his money and missed a sovereign and some silver; he then went out and afterwards saw Murrells go into a neighbouring house.[12]

Hannah was charged with the theft of £1 13s – the equivalent of six or seven weeks' wages for a factory girl – and Platford with receiving the money, and they both appeared at the Easter Quarter Sessions represented by a barrister, Mr Chambers, who managed the case effectively for his clients. Hannah took the blame for the crime, claiming Platford had nothing to do with it, and their attorney cleverly used some confusing circumstantial evidence around a dropped sovereign and Hannah's supposed feminine vulnerability (her assumption of guilt was apparently attributable 'not to real guilt but to fright') to persuade the jury that the drunken wheelwright was to blame for his misfortune and was mistaken about the money. Platford's previous record was not mentioned and the jury acquitted them.

In 1854 Hannah became pregnant with her first child, Thomas. When her next child, George, died in a domestic accident in 1859, aged 15 months, he was described at his inquest as 'the illegitimate son of Hannah Murrells of Maidenburgh Street'.[13] The year 1859 was not a good one for Platford either, as his neighbours and a parish overseer lodged a complaint against his house of ill fame. Luckily, the vestry did not wish to go to the expense of a court case and were content for the head constable to give a warning. Platford refused to heed the warning after taking legal advice and continued as before.[14] Co-incidentally, shortly afterwards, Thomas's brother William was cautioned for running a disorderly beerhouse in Wyre Street.

Hannah's next child was a daughter, born in 1860, whom she named Hannah. This choice of names for the eldest boy and girl suggests that Hannah was attempting respectability as a common-law wife, as naming children after their parents was a common practice in many families. When, in 1870, Thomas was accused of stealing a silver watch and Hannah with receiving it, she claimed to be his wife. But Hannah never would be Thomas's wedded wife and her children were Murrells until Thomas died, after which they swiftly changed their names to Platford. In 1886 Hannah described herself as Hannah Platford, widow.[15]

> COMPLAINT AGAINST A HOUSE OF ILL-FAME.—Mr. D. J. Dennis, one of the overseers of St. Nicholas, said he attended at the request of the vestry of that parish to make a complaint against a house of ill-fame in Maidenburgh Street, kept by a man named Thomas Platford. The parish wished to have it suppressed, and had applied to the landlady, but she had refused to interfere.— The MAYOR said cases of this description were very difficult to deal with. The course laid down by law was to indict the keeper of the house at the Quarter Session.—Mr. Dennis said the parish did not wish to go to any expense; and he suggested that the Magistrates might take summary measures.—Head-constable Downes said from complaints received he had visited the house, and Platford had promised to leave, but had since obtained legal advice, and defied them.—Mr Secrett, and a woman living next door, spoke to the great annoyance caused by the house.—The MAYOR said instructions would be given to the police, which he hoped would have the desired effect.—Mr. Dennis, after thanking the Bench, then withdrew.

Figure 8. The report on Platford's brothel in the *Essex Standard* (29 April 1859) demonstrating the difficulties involved in attempting to close down a brothel.

The censuses of 1861 and 1871 show that Thomas Platford and Hannah Murrells had not changed their livelihood. In 1861 they were still renting the 'well-built and roomy' house with a yard on the west side of Maidenburgh Street. At the next census they were in Williams Walk, a little street tucked into the back of the houses on the west side of Maidenburgh Street and which, conveniently situated near the market, had also been associated with prostitution for many years. The household included Hannah Murrells' four children. Thomas Platford gave his occupation as 'dealer' and 'general hawker' without specifying the commodity and Hannah, nearing her fortieth birthday, gave her occupation as tailoress. The census presents an innocuous household but other evidence shows the brothel was still in business, as shown below.

So Hannah's life as a prostitute progressed from the Union workhouse to a common law partnership and a family life with the notorious Thomas Platford, whose wild years were not yet behind him. The fact that she was under a man's protection (alternatively, that Thomas was living off her earnings) put her into a different category of prostitute from many of the others. She may even have become the brothel manager by this stage in her life. Notwithstanding Platford's record for theft, drunkenness and affray in Colchester, Hannah probably felt some level of security in her life. Although unmarried, she was living as a family; she knew that it was difficult for the authorities to close down a brothel if the parish was unwilling to bring its existence to court; and there is no evidence that Platford's drunken and violent behaviour was ever meted out on her. From her unpromising beginnings in the fields of Copford she had progressed to a brothel and a family life of sorts.

In 1870 Hannah and Thomas were again in trouble, charged with stealing a silver watch from a customer in the Blue Boar in Angel Lane. Thomas Green, a carpenter, had been at the bar enjoying his half pint when he was joined from another room by Thomas Platford and fellow hawker James Manning. When he realised his watch had gone he immediately accused them of taking it and shouted 'Police'. At this point Hannah Murrells 'rushed from the same room as the other prisoners came from and, pushing past him, declared that the prisoner Platford (who she stated was her husband) was innocent'. The watch was subsequently discovered in the yard and the case was dismissed, after an adjournment, for lack of proof.[16] But the case also demonstrated how easy it was for a man to be judged by the company he kept. The solicitor defending the prisoners suggested to Thomas Green that he had done a deal with Hannah Murrells. In Thomas Green's words, 'that if she said nothing about my sleeping with Hannah Green I would abandon these proceedings'. Thomas Green denied this accusation, which had no doubt originated from Hannah.[17]

This was at least the eleventh occasion on which Thomas Platford had been before the bench in the previous 30 years: four times for theft, twice for assault, twice as the victim of an assault, twice for drunkenness and once for debt. In addition, his brothel had three times been the subject of complaint. At the age of 50 he was well known to police and magistrates. His police record may explain why the case was brought on such circumstantial evidence and why it was prolonged for a week or more in the hope of gathering more evidence. The bench was clearly suspicious that Platford and Murrells were up to old tricks, yet the victim was apparently not above suspicion either.

Two years later, their brothel was under investigation by the coroner. A woman named Emma Boyden – 'a girl of loose character' – died suddenly 'at her lodgings in Williams Walk … a room at the house of a man named Thomas Platford'. Emma was born and brought up in Colchester, the eldest of five daughters of an umbrella maker who lived on North Hill. There is some evidence to suggest her mother Jemima may also have been a prostitute around the time of Emma's death. The problem was that the neighbourhood was suspicious, 'there being certain rumours with reference to the case' which were the reason the inquest was held. Emma's father reported that 'she told him just before she died that she had taken a certain drug some months ago to procure an abortion'. However, Dr George Brown was confident she had died of 'dropsy, brought on by impurity of blood, the result of former disease', no doubt a euphemism for acute syphilis, and the jury returned a verdict of natural causes. The *Standard* decided not to regale its readers with salacious details.[18] Thomas Platford had been in trouble with the borough police on many occasions but had usually managed to avoid a prison sentence. He had kept the brothel at the back of Maidenburgh Street with Hannah Murrells and her children for twenty years without any effective complaint being lodged by the parish and he died before the 1885 Act under which these brothel premises were cleared. However, the prolonged inquest held on Emma Boyden suggests an attempt was made by some of his neighbours to raise their disapproval in public one more time.

Some time after this event Thomas Platford moved his family to Stanwell Street and died there in 1876. In the same year Hannah's eldest son, Thomas, now a married man calling himself Platford rather than Murrells, produced Hannah's first grandchild. Hannah continued living in Stanwell Street as a tailoress with her two remaining children until they too married. Her sons Thomas and Frederick feature frequently in stories in the press. In 1886 Hannah was distressed when Thomas's wife Louisa ran off temporarily with another man. It was reported that Hannah 'did not care a penny about the disappearance of this worthless woman, but her grandchild, to whom she was very much attached, had also disappeared and … they did not know whether she was dead or alive'.[19] Louisa was later sentenced to a month in prison for assaulting Thomas.

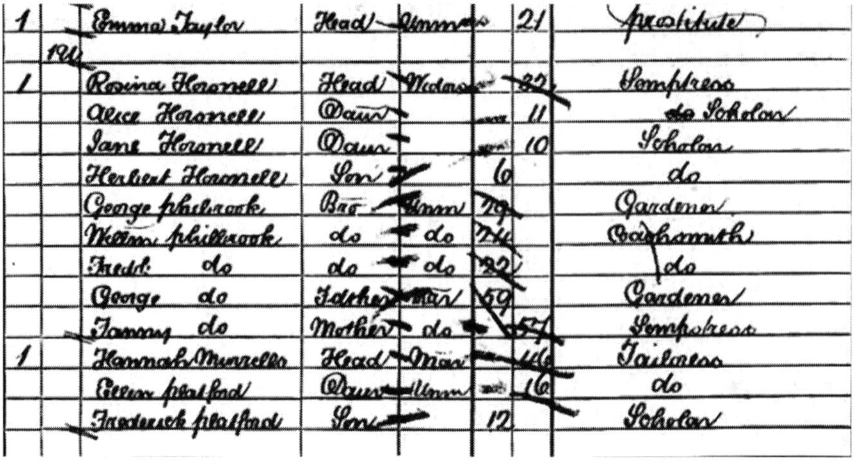

1	Emma Taylor	Head	Unm	21	Prostitute
1	Rosina Howell	Head	Widow	32	Sempstress
	Alice Howell	Daur		11	do Scholar
	Jane Howell	Daur		10	Scholar
	Herbert Howell	Son		6	do
	George Philbrook	Bro	Unm	29	Gardener
	William Philbrook	do	do	24	Blacksmith
	Fredk do	do	do	22	do
	George do	Father	Mar	59	Gardener
	Fanny do	Mother	do	57	Sempstress
1	Hannah Murrells	Head	Mar	46	Tailoress
	Ellen Platford	Daur	Unm	16	do
	Frederick Platford	Son		12	Scholar

Figure 9. A portion of the 1881 census for Stanwell Street. It shows Hannah Murrels living at No. 5 Stanwell Street with her two younger Platford children. Three doors away lived (Marmalade) Emma Taylor, who gave her occupation as prostitute.

In 1890 Hannah was served an order of ejectment from her home in Stanwell Street (see the opening quote to this chapter). She was 56 years old and referred to herself as Platford's widow. She contemplated a return to the vice trade. Her sons Frederick and Thomas got into a fight over Fred and his mother 'wanting to keep a certain class of house' that Thomas, a man raised in the brothel, 'strongly objected to'. This was Hannah's alternative to the Union, much as it had been when she was a girl. For a month or two she tried living with her son Thomas, but 'in consequence of his cruelty she was compelled to leave' and went into the Union.[20] She lived into her seventies and spent her final decade, as her childhood, as an inmate of the Union workhouse.

In some ways Hannah's life was exceptional among her peers. She stuck with Thomas Platford through thick and thin and, like a gangster's moll, was willing to take the blame for his misdeeds, a strategy that succeeded in defying the law on several occasions. In his many brushes with authority Thomas was exceedingly lucky in that he often evaded punishment, but he could also afford to hire attorneys who helped him achieve this outcome. His hawking, thieving and brothel keeping supported his family, but he and Hannah remained unmarried. We have not found any other unmarried prostitute with quite such a supportive attachment to her pimp. Hannah herself comes through in the sources as a feisty and undeferential female. She displayed naughty behaviour as a child in the workhouse. She gave her opinion freely – as shown in the story above concerning her son's wife – and was skilled at diverting attention when in a tight corner. She was unusual in that she was never arrested or charged with drunken disorder and, once she was with Platford, she also avoided prison. She must have valued her life in the brothel, as she hatched a plan to avoid old age in the Union by opening another brothel with her younger son, 'a man not given to working'. When her elder son vetoed this plan Hannah's options for independent living suddenly ended. The 1901 census reveals her at the age of 66 as an inmate of the Union workhouse.

Notes

1. *ES* 24 May 1890. Mrs Platford was Hannah Murrells' assumed name.
2. Fordham parish registers record her baptism on 6 July 1834. The 1841 census gives her birth year as 1835. The registers also show that there were three other Murrell families in Fordham.
3. *ES* 15 April 1864.
4. *ES* 19 January 1849. The story was headlined 'Union House Disorderlies'.
5. T. Apter, 'Pink and Blue', *Times Literary Supplement*, 12 March 2010, pp. 4–5.
6. Colchester set up a society to assist penitent females in 1840, but, with an income of £30 a year, it dealt with just 20 women in its first six years. The Sisters of Mercy home at Great Maplestead and Mrs Round's Female Refuge in the Ipswich Road, Colchester, did not open their doors until the 1860s.
7. *ES* 10 August 1849.
8. Subsequently renamed Military Road.
9. Subsequently renamed Vineyard Street.
10. In the 1851 census return Hannah's name is spelt Morral. In subsequent censuses it is spelt Murrells.
11. *ES* 11 January 1861.
12. *ES* 1 April 1853.
13. *ES* 30 November 1859.
14. The head constable said 'he had visited the house and Platford had promised to leave, but had since obtained legal advice and defied them'. *ES* 29 April 1859.
15. *ES* 26 June 1886.
16. *ES* 7 November 1870.
17. *ES* 11 November 1870.
18. *ES* 19 January 1872.
19. *ES* 26 June 1886.
20. *ES* 26 July 1890.

CHAPTER 4

Men who encouraged prostitution

*A more respectable man never put
his feet into a pair of boots.*[1]

As the example of Thomas Platford in the last chapter shows, men played an essential role in enabling and supporting Colchester's vice trade. They fell into three groups: firstly, the prostitutes' customers; secondly, the men who employed prostitutes in brothels, public houses and beerhouses, and who, to that extent, could be said partially to live off immoral earnings; and, thirdly, a group (that also included some property-owning women) who rented premises to prostitutes and brothel keepers but who kept their distance, merely pocketing their rent without asking how it was earned. All these men could be said to be involved in the trade as, in their different ways, they all ensured that prostitution flourished and for the purposes of this chapter they are all presented as men who encouraged prostitution, whether their profiting was done blatantly or covertly.

Members of the third group, when called to account, usually excused themselves on the grounds of ignorance. They claimed that the tenant of the property seemed to be respectable, perhaps said she was married or was accompanied by a man whom she claimed was her husband. Members of the second group were sometimes confrontational when called to account, taking the line that prostitution was not illegal and that the girls had to have premises to work from. The first group relied on the prevailing double standard – defined as a rule of good behaviour that some, but not all, are expected to follow. Under this rule it was acceptable for men to excuse themselves on the grounds of having been tricked in some way by a prostitute and to present themselves as innocent dupes. Within the context of a paternalistic and Christian society such excuses were well-founded – as Adam said of Eve, 'the woman tempted me and I did eat'.[2] The woman's wiles, which, by definition, were inscrutable to the man, explained his lapse of morality. The concept of entrapment put the blame for the property owner's and the customer's temporary lapse firmly on the woman. While the law remained weak (before 1885), the authorities supported this cultural double standard. But it is undeniable that some of the stories, especially the ones involving soldier customers, strongly suggest that, at best, most prostitution transactions were made freely and willingly by both parties. Our sources also suggest, male excuses notwithstanding, that there were encounters in which prostitutes took advantage of men when they were drunk or sleeping off a sexual encounter.

We do not have much evidence of individual men operating in more than one of the above categories at different times. No men wealthy enough to have property to let were caught *in flagrante* by a constable in Colchester who then proceeded to a charge. If there were brothels for middle-class men in Colchester they managed to keep below the radar and were not reported in the press. The British Hotel (below) may be one example of such a brothel. Most men involved in the trade were working men with wives and families who, like many of the prostitutes, also had a respectable day job, but a few were citizens of some social or professional standing in the town. Our database has the names and details of 121 men whose names were associated with prostitution. Of these, 54 per cent were customers, 26 per cent were landlords (most of public houses or beerhouses but a few of privately rented premises) and 14 per cent lived with prostitutes as pimp or paramour. The remainder were linked with individual prostitutes in one-off escapades.

The prostitutes' customers

The customer group accounts for just over half of the men in the database and more than half of *them* were military. The *Essex Standard* printed a letter in February 1856, just a month after the arrival of the first soldiers.

> It appears that most indecorous and improper conduct on the part of a number of soldiers (amounting almost to a riot) took place on Friday last outside the Factory, from a number of soldiers waiting for the girls to come out and then assailing them in a most improper and indecent manner. With regard to the Girls' Ragged School, some of the soldiers have been guilty of similar conduct on a smaller and less obnoxious scale.[3]

These soldiers were clearly proactive customers, actively seeking willing women whatever the police and magistrates may have suspected about their 'entrapment' by prostitutes and beerhouses; however, civilian men may have been 'entrapped' in such a manner, as there are several stories in which it appears that the woman targeted an apparently unsuspecting man. For instance, David Keeble, a Colchester man who was transporting army baggage for the 5th Dragoon Guards from Colchester to Aldershot, said he fell in with a Stratford prostitute, bought her several drinks and took a walk with her before he missed his purse, containing over £7. Keeble presents his story as a victim who 'fell' rather than an active participant who agreed to a woman's invitation.[4] George Willsmer, another example, was a farm bailiff who came to Colchester to cash a cheque to pay the harvestmen. He claimed that

> on walking near the Plough Inn, St Botolph's Street, he was accosted by a female, whom he accompanied to some fields near the Camp and there fell asleep. On waking he discovered himself minus about £15. 10 in gold which was previously safe in his pocket; and the girl too was *non est*.[5]

Clearly neither Willsmer nor the newspaper was inclined to divulge every detail of the encounter, but it seems unlikely that he and the unknown female who 'accosted' him were just going to the fields for a friendly chat in the heat of a July afternoon. It is much more likely that Willsmer was using the concept of entrapment to avoid taking responsibility for his own failure of common sense.[6] If the man in question was a youth the bench sometimes pointed out his folly in such cases. James Marriage, a wheelwright in his twenties, was 'in company' one Saturday night with a prostitute who stole his purse containing eleven shillings. He decided to take her to court where, in addition to his financial loss, he also had to endure being 'reprimanded by the bench for his conduct on the occasion'.[7] Occasionally the bench seems to have felt that theft was somehow mitigated by prostitution. When private Frederick Bartliff found his pockets had been rifled by the prostitute he went to bed with, the chairman of the bench, Dr Duncan, told him the punishment of the girl was 'mitigated in consequence of the immoral consequences under which the robbery was committed and the temptation (he) had given to the prisoner' – in other words, *caveat emptor*.[8]

Money was at the root of almost all the prostitutes' encounters with their customers. Most were simple transactions, both parties getting what they wanted and moving on without drawing attention to themselves. In Chapter 2 we discussed the inadequate wages of working girls and the difficulties they had in gaining financial independence. Colchester's working men seem to have been paid about twice the woman's wage and tradesmen were sometimes recorded earning more than £1 a week. Although we have few records of what Colchester's prostitutes were paid for their sex work it is unlikely that their customers would have been able or willing to pay much for their sexual encounters. When Sarah Ann Abbott took Henry Wetney, 'a labouring man', home he gave her a shilling and she then stole his purse.[9]

But in some cases the details contained in the court records and newspaper reports suggest that quite complex monetary transactions could develop around prostitution. For instance, some soldiers seem to have borrowed money from prostitutes and also to have relied on them to keep or hide their money for periods of time – both money that was honestly come by as gifts and legacies and money that had been stolen. There was no arrangement in the barracks that allowed private soldiers to keep valuables safely and many of the soldiers were at a distance from family on whom they might have relied to look after spare cash. Corporal Gray charged Elizabeth Alger with stealing his money. He had obtained furlough to enable him to go to Ireland but had, instead, come to Colchester to see Elizabeth and to 'give her some money to take care of. She however went off to Ipswich and spent it.'[10] In another case Sarah Avey, who lived in Eld Lane, received a visit one afternoon from two soldiers who demanded money. When she refused, one held her down while the other took her purse and some jewellery. In court the soldier explained that Sarah had 'had his regimental pay for months past and that he did not consider that he was stealing the money. He gave [Sarah] the money to pay for the locket and chain.'[11] In both of these cases the soldier customer was characterising his relationship with the prostitute as something more personal and enduring and also developing the monetary transaction he had with her in new ways. These and other soldiers in several similar cases seemed to think that their having regularly paid for sex with a chosen prostitute allowed them to make certain financial assumptions, such as calling on her to lend them cash or to keep their deposits of cash in safe keeping. But in all such cases that came to court the woman was actively rejecting this male assumption, in some cases because she had failed to keep her side of any deal. As we saw in Chapter 2, some soldiers proceeded to marry a prostitute, so perhaps these additional monetary arrangements were a prelude to courtship for some.

Theft was another kind of monetary transaction associated with prostitution. Most of the civilian customers in the following account have been identified because the prostitute stole from them. Most of the thefts were of substantial sums of money or valuable property. Soldiers stole prostitutes' property quite as often as prostitutes stole theirs and sometimes soldiers used prostitutes to hide, fence or pawn stolen property. They were caught stealing a third party's goods together less frequently. In a case that was reported at great length in the *Standard*, probably because the police had used some ingenuity in catching the miscreants, Private Bromley and two friends arrived at the Crown and Anchor in Stanwell Street early one Saturday morning. Charlotte Smith, a prostitute, was on duty, and Bromley 'gave her four half sovereigns to take care of, saying he was going to Ipswich and would be back that night or next morning'. Another soldier 'gave her a sovereign to get a coat and trousers; and she afterwards fetched a waistcoat, collar and scarf for him' from a second-hand clothing shop. While she was out attending to this commission she also 'went to the butcher's for four pounds of steak for Bromley', which she cooked, and they all sat down to breakfast together. The money originated in a robbery committed on a fellow soldier and when the men moved off to catch the Ipswich train Charlotte and another prostitute accompanied them and the whole gang was arrested.[12] It is clear from the way this story was told that although Charlotte had not technically robbed anyone the fact that she had willingly spent the proceeds of a robbery on behalf of her customers made her complicit. The story also involved a fellow prostitute, Ann Goodwin, who was asked by one of the soldiers to 'get change for half a sovereign', which she did at a local shop. The monetary transactions in this story were allied to prostitution but only indirectly, in that the women involved were prostitutes: the men were actually buying a hearty breakfast rather than a sexual encounter and the prostitutes were enabling the soldiers to spend stolen money in alternative pleasurable ways that involved them, such as a day out in Ipswich.

In another example, Ellen Gould was charged under the Mutiny Act with possessing War Department property (a pair of brushes). Under questioning she said the property had been given to her by a soldier who told her it was his own and that when she questioned him 'on one occasion he knocked her down and threatened to kill her if she said any more about [it]'.[13] Although the bench expressed disbelief that Ellen could have been so naïve, her sentence was lenient.

There are a number of accounts of encounters between a prostitute and a customer that involved violence and aggression: the man assaulting, or being assaulted by, a prostitute, often in broad daylight (an example of the latter is given in the final chapter). For example, Florence Burrows was found by the police in an unconscious state 'suffering from severe contusions to the face and chest ... she said she had been with two soldiers in the Gardener's Arms and that they afterwards knocked her down and kicked her about the chest and face, and then ran away'.[14] Prostitute Edith Churchyard refused to take a soldier indoors, whereupon he 'struck her on the nose, causing the blood to flow, knocked her down and kicked her about the body'.[15] Other instances involve a man, or a group of men, helping the woman to resist arrest. Some of these aggressive encounters were to do with failed monetary transactions, but others were in response to an insult delivered by the woman. Consorting with prostitutes risked exposing the customer to public view both at the time and also in the magistrates' court. Street disorders in which a large group of soldiers and women assembled together, often to adjudicate a female fight or disagreement, were also a focus of aggression. Since most female fights did not take place on the street, but in a bar or a lodging house, such encounters are more like the pre-arranged fights between men such as took place regularly in Osborne Street.[16] The women swore like troopers, were free with their fists when affronted and shouted their grievances for all to hear.

In addition, a combination of the soldiers' outdoor way of life (and their duty to be corralled in barracks at night) and the girls' overcrowded living conditions seems to have encouraged a vagrant kind of prostitution, referred to in police statements as 'flattening the corn' – just as, as already noted, there are examples of civilian customers taking prostitutes into fields. Ellen Southernwood, just one of many examples, was initially picked up 'among some shrubs' on the Abbey Field one Sunday morning in August 1890. She was sleeping alongside a corporal of the Norfolk regiment and another couple. Sometimes the act took place in the street, as when Mary Ann Golding was charged with indecency 'in the thoroughfare leading by the Camp wall from Mersea Road to Military Road'. A witness had seen her there 'behaving indecently with a soldier. It was a great nuisance by night and day to persons living there.'[17] It is possible that the customers taking advantage of alfresco brothels were merely enjoying summer nights or a reduced rate, but they ran the risk of being arrested for indecency or vagrancy if caught. This kind of behaviour was a major challenge to that section of the law-abiding population who were anxious to affirm the growing politeness of the town but reticent about making intolerant formal complaints.

Encounters with prostitutes were usually blamed for a man's diagnosis of venereal disease. We have already given an account of the numbers afflicted in the garrison and why this was seen to be a problem in need of a solution. Civilians afflicted with venereal disease were not counted in this way before the twentieth century, so information on them is harder to find. A sad inquest case was reported in Colchester in 1850 involving a 21-year-old pork butcher's son who was taking mercury – the remedy of choice for syphilis – which made him feel unwell, in addition to loosening all his teeth. Unwilling to confide in a surgeon or in his mother on the grounds that 'it would break her heart', he took the medical advice of a prostitute, who said she had known him for several years. He died of respiratory failure with opium in his pocket. The coroner did not question the origin of his ailment, which (assuming he was not born with the condition) can only have been a syphilitic prostitute, but he did question whether he had intended to end his life. The sympathetic jurors decided he took opium to get some sleep and that the overdose was inadvertent, but a long discussion then took place about the medical conduct of the post-mortem, in the process diverting the attention well away from the subject of syphilis to the science of detecting opium poisoning and the ability of Colchester's medics to arrive at a satisfactory conclusion as to cause of death.[18]

Most men chose to present themselves as simple victims and the newspaper sometimes reported embarrassed laughter and an air of masculine indulgence for foolish youth when their cases came up in court. Private Bolger was entertaining prostitute Rebecca Gorman in the New Market Tavern when she 'ran away with his carpet bag'. In court the next morning, still somewhat

Many of Colchester's beerhouses provided premises for prostitution and case studies of two premises in Magdalen Street are given in Chapter 5. Such brothels were usually next door or very close to the beerhouse, but outside its premises, so that they could continue in business should the alcohol licence be lost. Most beerhouses were small domestic premises but a few were larger public houses that had been downgraded through the loss of their spirit licence. Colchester had no red-light district as such. Its many pubs and beerhouses were spread throughout the town and about half of them were named at least once in events concerning prostitutes. Once the garrison had arrived at least a quarter of them came in for criticism on one or more of the annual licensing days for being disorderly haunts, as described in detail in later chapters. As one magistrate described this trade: 'the low public house and the brothel are too frequently found to be not far apart, and sometimes their seductions are combined'.[25] The beerhouse landlords were not often accused of *harbouring* prostitutes, as they employed some of them as servants and let out rooms to others for a fee, either for a weekly rent or ad hoc. If the woman was a servant and/or a lodger she was not vulnerable to the law that allowed prostitutes to spend only enough time to satisfy their immediate refreshment needs in the pub or beerhouse. This meant that the servant–prostitutes were free to come and go, as shown in the case of Charlotte Smith (above). Colchester's prostitutes had a tendency to congregate and to solicit in beerhouses, whether they were working there or not. Pettinger, in her account of modern prostitution, suggests that customers preferred the prostitute to present a 'work self', such as a server of food or drink, as this tended to obscure the market transaction centred on the sex act. She also quotes Wolkowitz, who argues that prostitution is not the only female pursuit that involves 'body work': so too do modelling, lap dancing and waitressing. 'The contentious moral standing of sex work should not prevent comparison between sex work and other forms of body work.'[26] Some of Colchester's beerhouse prostitutes were expected to serve drinks to customers and, because the women and the soldiers and other customers were frequently drunk, violence could erupt in the bar, the yard and the rooms above.

Most of the disreputable premises were ostensibly run by men who, like the prostitutes, also had a day job, such as cobbler or dealer. Most were married and the wife carried on the business during the husband's absences and also often took the blame for irregularities such as serving drink outside the permitted hours. Most beerhouse tenants were contracted by one of Colchester's several brewing firms under a variety of arrangements usually organised by the brewer's agent. Tenancies ranged from weekly to annual agreements and some remuneration deals were linked to the sale of beer. When problems arose the brewer was never held to account, being shielded from scrutiny by one of the town's solicitors. Occasionally a letter to the press would blame the power of the brewing industry for the town's woes, but even temperance society meetings generally focused their attention on the pub rather than the brewer. The brewers' agents were instructed to remove a landlord in danger of losing the licence, but the incoming landlord might continue the prostitution trade unabated for several years before he too was replaced. As we shall see in later chapters, magistrates and solicitors had a repertoire of clichés to do with the rights of working men to enjoy the pleasures of the beer house and the acceptable existence of 'low' neighbourhoods where authoritarian policing would be inadvisable. This was a strong message delivered in public, particularly in the years when the bench felt under pressure to explain why it did not refuse licence applications. Nevertheless, despite these claims, beerhouse brothels were not restricted to 'low' neighbourhoods in Colchester.

Whatever the particulars of the brewer–landlord contract, beerhouses were difficult businesses to run. Chapters 5 and 10 are case studies of licensed premises which made provision for prostitution. From close reading of the police evidence presented in court in the context of prostitution it seems clear that the police were instructed to act carefully, if possible persuading all those involved to keep a low profile. It is also clear that the police did not tolerate breaches of the peace, including threatening behaviour towards the police; so, if the beerhouse landlord could control the disorderly aspect of the business his licence was not in jeopardy.

John Hunter kept a beerhouse near the top of West Stockwell Street for over 20 years. He was born in 1820 and apparently began his working life as groom and valet to Lord Panmure.[27] After nine and a half years he became a travelling tea dealer, selling his round in 1851 to become a shopkeeper in Colchester. The shop was variously described as a coffee shop (1851), an eating house (1861), a beerhouse and hairdresser's (1863) and an inn, having been granted a spirit licence in 1870 after several years of applications. In 1869 his beerhouse acquired a name – the British Hotel. In 1871 Hunter was also described as a horse dealer and, in 1877, as a moneylender. The details of his complicated and precarious business life were presented at regular intervals in the borough county court, to which, throughout his working life in Colchester, he resorted several times a year to obtain money owed to him or to answer accusations of business chicanery by aggrieved complainants. But there was no mention of prostitution in his house through all these years. Mr Hunter, whose customers were farmers, dealers and market traders, increasingly prospered in trade and kept close control of his bar and bedrooms. He was so confident that he came to the borough court to lodge a complaint after the *Essex Gazette* reported that absconding apprentices had been found in his house with some girls: 'anyone who read this statement … would naturally suppose he kept a house of bad repute'.[28] But he seems to have lost his touch in the mid-1870s, after the

TO BE LET,
WITH EARLY POSSESSION,

THE ARTILLERY ARMS, MAIDENBURGH STREET, COLCHESTER. The above well-known Beer, Ale, Porter, and Stout House, situate a few yards from High Street, one of the main thoroughfares, contains a spacious Dancing Saloon, which has the support of the Military and Civilians of the town. The adjoining premises can be hired with the above, by which means the business of a Lodging-House may be advantageously added; an opportunity thus offers itself for a lucrative business. Rent low, and valuation moderate to a suitable tenant.

Apply to the present Proprietor, or the Stores, Cross Keys, Colchester.

Figure 12. This advertisement appeared on the front page of the *Essex Standard* in February 1867. The innocuous 'lodging house' could so easily be transformed into a brothel by a profiteering tenant.

business of prostitution flourished. Charles Neville, prosecuted for allowing prostitutes to work at the Colchester Arms (see above), moved on to the Mermaid in Mersea Road, a beerhouse described in 1869 as 'the pest of the neighbourhood'.[39] In 1871 Ben Firmin and his wife were brought to book for their brothel in Pelham's Lane (see Chapter 8). In addition to these notorious cases, prostitutes were associated with many other beerhouses. The women were rarely arrested *in* the licensed premises, but their stories nevertheless include mentions of a further 40 establishments, some of them many times. Topping the list are the Lifeboat (nine times 1874–89), the Anchor (six times 1856– 92) and the Woolpack (five times 1856–90).

Pubs and beerhouses provided special facilities such as dancing rooms and musicians, as well as serving girls, to lure their customers. An advertisement was placed in the *Essex Standard* on 6 February 1867. The Artillery Arms in Maidenburgh Street, 'situate[d] a few yards from High Street', was to let (see above). The alcohol licence did not include the lodging house, thus allowing the brothel to flourish in the unlikely event of the licence being revoked. The magistrates sometimes complained about the deliberate 'entrapment' of soldiers and the harbouring of young girls in such places, but more frequently they accepted the complacent – or realistic – view that low neighbourhoods bred low public houses. 'We all know the character of garrison towns, and we all know that where there are soldiers there will be camp followers', as the mayor said on the annual licensing meeting in 1867.[40] The police concurred.

In 1867, when a member of the public lodged a complaint with the bench that Abbeygate Street and St John's Green were sites of frequent disturbances, the mayor recommended that the police should take action, but the head constable said 'when the persons were spoken to by the police they generally went away and there the matter ended'.[41]

The beerhouses protected their prostitutes as well as they could. The Abbeygate suffered nine broken windows after its landlord refused an aggrieved soldier permission to go upstairs to find the girl who had robbed him of his money when he lay sleeping upon a settle.[42] But there are also many accounts of prostitutes being assaulted by their customers outside the beerhouse. Victoria Butcher lived in the brothel adjoining Paddy's Goose in Vineyard Street. When she entered a friend's room one night she found a soldier there alone who went for her with a knife.[43] In June 1866 a soldier assaulted Eliza Clover in Vineyard Street, breaking her jaw with a kick; she had 'used some offensive expression' to him before the attack. Six months previously Susannah Golding was punched to the ground in the High Street by a farrier from the 17th Lancers. His excuse? 'She was intoxicated and had some of the prisoner's money.' Soldiers used their belts, their boots, their fists and knives to inflict injury. So, while some soldier customers preferred to set up a cohabitation arrangement for as long as they were in the town, others had a dangerous and violent approach to the women, especially when drunk.

It was very unusual for the court or the newspaper to report men for living off immoral earnings, although the words 'paramour' and 'cohabit' were occasionally used with that implication. Because, prior to 1885, the law was weak concerning brothel clearance, the system worked to reduce the effect of vice rather than to attempt to remove it (as explained in later chapters). The police were not keen to arrest prostitutes if they could persuade them to go home quietly and they were even less keen to arrest brothel keepers in the period before 1885.

Prostitutes' landlords

The third group of men profiting from prostitution were the property owners who rented out houses to prostitutes. These cases came to court only after the 1885 change in the law that gave the police, rather than the parish authorities, the power to close brothels. In 1886 Colchester's police took the opportunity offered by the new law to bring the owners of two such premises to court and expose the respectable property owners to public scrutiny. Mr Charles Wire, described as a retired tradesman but also a Methodist preacher, was charged with allowing his property in Childwell Alley to be used as a brothel by girls of ill fame. During the case, which 'excited considerable interest', the head constable paid lip service to Mr

Wire's 'respectability and advanced age', while refuting the idea that he could possibly have remained ignorant of the reputation of the property and the tenants. He found a witness who had warned Mr Wire that 'his barracks were full of men'. He produced details of his prostitute tenants who had been convicted for disorderly conduct and he reported that the houses had a long history as brothels and were a constant source of complaint owing to the disgraceful scenes that occurred there.

However, the constable was no match for the defending solicitor, Mr Asher Prior, who produced a technical objection 'that it had not been proved that either of these houses was a brothel ... set apart for purposes of prostitution'. In order to prove this the police should have kept watch outside the premises, counting the customers in and out, as they learned to do in subsequent cases. The bench seized on the significance of this point and dismissed the case, although they supported the head constable's actions and stated that 'the houses should be more respectably tenanted'. It seems that the magistrates were caught between a wish to shield the respectable owner of the property and a wish to be seen to be responding to the new law. Mr Prior then rose to his feet and made a statement that his client Mr Wire objected to being let off on a technical objection.

> His client wished him to say that during his whole long life of 76 years he had never been before any court of justice upon any charge whatever. He was brother to a former Lord Mayor of London, he had been a subscriber to Mrs Round's Refuge for many years, and he had also been a local preacher in connection with the Wesleyan Methodists for nearly half a century and he certainly was unaware that these girls were of such a character.

Mr Wire, who died two years later aged 78, is logged in every census from 1841 to 1881. He lived and traded as a baker and tea dealer in Magdalen Street and retired to an almshouse around the corner in Military Road, where he lived with his second wife and a servant girl. Either he was an exceptionally tolerant man – he responded to the 'barracks' warning by saying 'that the girls paid him the rent and as long as they did that he should not trouble' himself about such advice – or he was an innocent victim of the women's manipulative tricks. His excuse in court was the latter – that he was 'unaware that these girls were of such a character. Two of them hired the place as married women and the other two had notice to quit when their character was ascertained but they refused to go out on the ground that the notice was only verbal.'[44] Clearly Mr Wire was in an embarrassing position, exposed as a hypocrite – a Methodist preacher who profited from prostitution – and vulnerable to additional accusations of venality and foolish ignorance. Attack, coupled with a diligent public service record, was his successful defence. The fact that the magistrates let him off and also allowed his statement to be heard is telling. Attitudes to prostitution were rarely black and white, as attested by many examples in the sources we have used. Tolerant attitudes were expressed by men at all social levels, and included comments that the girls must work somewhere and that they could not work without premises.

After Charles Wire's death his solicitor Mr Prior bought his Childwell Alley properties. As landlord, Mr Prior evidently began with good intentions, but when he attempted to smarten up the houses he encountered some local resistance. Stones shattered the newly painted windows, thrown, apparently, by one Ishmael Clark, a local pimp with a vicious reputation who had done the deed in the company of 'a lot of soldiers'.[45] Charles Wire's houses were not so easily gentrified. When they came up for scrutiny nine years later, Mr Prior explained that he had begun by clearing out the bad tenants, admitting that 'at the time of the purchase they were mostly filled with bad tenants, the greater part ... unfortunates, and the others ... not in the habit of paying their rents'. But the rents became 'troublesome to collect and for that reason [he] authorized the entire property to be let to Mrs Mary Cornish for one rental'. In other words, he employed Mrs Cornish to manage the tenants and collect the rents on his behalf. When he had enquired about bad tenants she had always reassured him. He claimed not to know that Mrs Cornish and her husband ran a brothel at Barn Yard in Magdalen Street in addition to being a rent collector for respectable landlords. Her skill as an evasive witness in this case was second to none.[46]

These Childwell Alley brothels demonstrate both the simplicity and the complexity of the business arrangements that were their foundation. It was a simple matter to rent one's property using an agent to collect the rental so that any bothersome details could be ignored. If the rent came in regularly the landlord did not ask awkward questions and the potentially exploitative relationship between the rent collector and the tenant was of no concern to him. Since the brothel manager was not usually the owner of the property it was difficult (before the 1885 Act) for the authorities to do more than occasionally expose the owners to public view and accept their protestations of ignorance or innocence.

Some brothels seemed to have made a lot of trouble for their neighbours. Most of Colchester's streets were already unduly noisy thanks to the efforts of drunken men and women trying to find their way home after a night out. The police dealt with shouting, swearing and fighting on a regular basis and seem always to have attempted to steer the noisy parties home rather than to the cells. The garrison provided a nocturnal picket to clear drunken soldiers out of the beerhouses at closing time and help them safely back to barracks. But, in addition to this commotion, some of the brothels also seem to have generated considerable extra noise. In a brothel-clearance case in Burlington Road in 1887, the neighbour living opposite complained of 'noises and uproar coming from that house'. The police constable, called to quell the noise, turned two soldiers out, but 'a great shrieking and smashing' followed at the back of the house.[47] Florence Garnham had her windows in Maidenburgh Street smashed by soldiers when she refused to let them in to escape the picket. Ellen George's neighbours in Bretts Buildings, Magdalen Street, reported seeing a soldier nearly killed in the brothel's back yard by a woman and three civilians wielding a hand brush, a table leg and a shoe. On another occasion soldiers got into this same brothel by a window 'and the row was kept up until two or three o'clock in the morning'. All of these cases feature brothels where the women managed their own business. Those run by a manager seem to have been more successful at controlling disorderly customers.

Conclusions

Finnegan argues that, in York, despite three-quarters of the prostitutes' customers being working-class men, prostitution was class exploitation: employers 'caused' prostitution because they paid below-subsistence wages.[48] The same argument could, of course, be made for Colchester, but whether higher wages would have changed working-class men's exploitation of women is debatable. Most feminist writers agree that female poverty was the basis of prostitution, so higher wages for women might well have reduced the supply of casual prostitutes. In garrison towns, such as York and Colchester, the presence of large numbers of single men increased the level of aggression on the streets. Prostitutes, just like their customers, also exhibited competitive and aggressive behaviour in public. The police described several encounters of prostitutes 'fighting like cats' and we give several examples in this account of prostitutes inflicting injuries on each other.

Although the men who had closest contact with Colchester's prostitutes as customers and brothel keepers were all working-class, those who owned the properties used for prostitution were generally of a somewhat higher social status. Before 1885 nothing could be done effectively to prevent property owners from allowing their premises to be used as brothels. The occasional damage to property caused by aggrieved customers was compensated by the ability of prostitutes to pay their rent. Most property owners seem to have felt that they were supporting working girls by providing them with premises. The rest claimed they had been deceived by females who pretended to be respectable tailoresses or married women.

Prostitution was not illegal provided it was done behind closed doors. But, as has already been suggested, it was hazardous for both parties as they preyed on each other through soliciting, aggressive rejections and theft of property;

considerable social skills were necessary to negotiate a mutually satisfactory transaction. For this reason third parties became involved as enablers and profiteers. Some, such as Thomas Platford, seem to have managed the brothel business successfully but others, such as Ishmael Clark, used intimidation to control women and his business did not endure for long. These individuals were vulnerable at law if the parish authorities chose to take action and those running licensed premises would also be in trouble on the annual licensing day should the police make a case against them. One way of avoiding this unwelcome police attention may have been through making informal payments, although we have only found one likely example of this. In 1913 the *Essex Newsman* reported a story with the headline 'Colchester Widow's Hoard'. Mrs Taylor, the aged widow of one of the policemen attached to the lock hospital, had died in the cottage they had shared in Military Road. More than £1,000 was discovered 'hidden away in unsuspected places in the dwelling'.[49] This was an enormous sum of money for a humble policeman to have amassed from his earnings and the fact that it was carefully hidden in his unpretentious cottage lays him open to the suspicion that he may have taken bribes from the prostitutes he was employed to confine under the CDAs.

However, it is also clear that these businesses, including property rentals, were protected by the prevailing capitalist and paternalistic culture until the last decade of the century. Police and magistrates were unwilling to deal harshly with those who earned a living, unless that living was built on theft of property. Men who earned their living as 'dealers' dealt in a variety of commodities from time to time and prostitution could easily be part of a dealer's portfolio. Reformers were also not inclined to level specific accusations, preferring to cloak their disapproval in moralistic generalities. It was only when the lock hospital system was disbanded in the 1880s, thanks to the vociferous anti-CDAs campaign, that serious attention turned away from prostitutes as the cause of the problem and towards the men (and women) who organised and profited from the trade. One result of the 1885 Criminal Amendment Act was that the police had to learn how to penetrate a culture of what the head constable termed 'shuffling excuses' so that the unwillingness publicly to blame men for the negative results of prostitution could be challenged. In order to bring a brothel clearance case to a successful conclusion in court they had to produce evidence that the solicitors found difficult to refute. So they spent longer watching premises and noting movements in and out of brothels, but they also spent time trying to persuade the women to decamp.

It was unusual for nineteenth-century men such as clergymen, doctors, solicitors and magistrates commenting on prostitution to blame men for the trade. They were more likely to see their gender as the victim of predatory women. One reason for this, apart from nineteenth-century double standards, was that the medical profession felt women were controlled by their reproductive systems and that women were the conduit for venereal disease.[50] Some also blamed the fashion for late marriage among middle-class men which was often caused by the need to command an income sufficient to attract a woman of his social status. Professional men were often well into their thirties before they attained this goal. Colchester's prostitutes served working-class men whose behaviour was seen by middle-class men to be 'weak and foolish rather than sinful'.[51] In other words, they had been led astray, albeit when under the influence of alcohol. But working-class men were quite often reported showing violence towards women, both verbal and physical, and this tendency increased markedly with the arrival of large numbers of soldiers in Colchester. As we showed in Chapter 2, most of the town's prostitutes solicited in beerhouses, many of which were attached to brothels, and the strong link between alcohol and prostitution allowed some of the elite to attack the pub rather than the brothel.

Notes

1. Mrs Woods, Annie Smith's landlady, referring ironically to prostitute Annie's intended husband. *ES* 26 November 1892.
2. Genesis 3:12.
3. *ES* 6 February 1856. The letter writer seems to have been most worried about the female schoolteachers' feelings. There were a number of middle-class ladies in Colchester who felt the factory girls were worthy of special attention too and, perhaps, during their evening events, which featured education both practical and moral and singing followed by tea and cakes, directions would have been given about how to deal with such attempts on feminine virtue.
4. *ES* 29 May 1868.
5. *ES* 27 July 1859.
6. The police apprehended 'notorious prostitute' Eliza Evans for this theft when she and her pimp were seen 'spending money freely in the town'. *ES* 27 July 1859.
7. *ES* 21 November 1855.
8. *ES* 29 April 1859.
9. *IJ* 6 May 1869.
10. In court the corporal changed his mind and declined to press charges, and Elizabeth was released. *ES* 4 December 1868.
11. *ES* 17 June 1882.
12. The head constable 'detailed the way in which Sgt Stewart ... cleverly laid hold on one of the prisoners at the Colchester Railway Station and telegraphed to stop the others, who went on by train to Ipswich, which was done'. *ES* 25 October 1867.
13. *ES* 17 May 1867.
14. *ES* 13 August 1887.
15. *ES* 11 November 1893.
16. An anonymous letter claimed that over 1,000 men, women and children had attended a fight in Osborne Street in a ring 'stuck out by flags'. *ES* 28 August 1857.
17. *ES* 22 July 1868.
18. A juror had complained about the need for two medical men at the inquest and the (medical)

coroner defended his decision at great length. *ES* 1 February 1850.
19 *ES* 21 May 1869.
20 *ES* 24 March 1871.
21 *ES* 17 April 1886.
22 *ES* 1 and 8 August 1885.
23 *ES* 7 April 1871. Sam Howe had earlier served a sentence for abusing his wife.
24 *ES* 13 October 1871.
25 *ES* 28 September 1866.
26 L. Pettinger, '"Knows how to please a man"; studying customers to understand service work', *The Sociological Review*, 59/2 (2011), pp. 223–41; C. Wolkowitz, *Bodies at Work* (London, 2006).
27 The *Essex Standard* refers to him by a variety of names – John Hunter, Doctor Hunter, Doctor Brown Hunter and Mr Hunter.
28 *ES* 14 January 1870. The hotel had 15 rooms, 11 beds and stabling for 12 horses.
29 *ES* 20 December 1879.
30 *ES* 27 July 1877 and 2 November 1877.
31 *ES* 15 February 1865.
32 *ES* 10 September 1869.
33 *ES* 7 February 1866.
34 *ES* 26 December 1866.
35 *ES* 17 October 1891.
36 *ES* 8 July 1853.
37 *ES* 30 March 1859.
38 *ES* 29 July 1857.
39 *ES* 31 March 1869.
40 *ES* 4 September 1867.
41 *ES* 23 January 1867.
42 *ES* 30 August 1867.
43 *ES* 10 September 1869.
44 *ES* 13 November 1886. The *Essex Telegraph* of the same date gave more specific details, the head constable saying that Childwell Alley was 'notorious for bad brothels' and the witness who had alerted Mr Wire to the nature of his tenants noting that Mr Wire had responded aggressively.
45 *ES* 14 May 1887.
46 Prostitute Annie Harris gave evidence against Mrs Cornish from her bed in the Infirmary. She said she lived with Mrs Cornish at the Barn Yard for 4s 1d rental per week. *ES* 6 April 1895.
47 *ES* 16 July 1887.
48 Finnegan, *Poverty and Prostitution*.
49 *Essex Newsman* 3 May 1913.
50 Lee, *Policing Prostitution*; Kent, *Sex and Suffrage*.
51 Finnegan, *Poverty and Prostitution*, pp. 8 and 118.

CHAPTER 5

The Lifeboat and The Anchor

*The house was a funny
one when he took it on.*[1]

This chapter presents a case study of a beerhouse and a public house situated on opposite sides of Magdalen Street, both of which were in business for some or all of our period. Both of these premises were involved in prostitution in an area of the town that was poor, overcrowded and associated with anti-social behaviour. The difficulties their landlords dealt with and the solutions they found when in trouble demonstrate some of the issues involved in trading in this part of town. Some of the difficulties were of the landlords' own making, to do with criminality, but others were more to do with crowd control.

Magdalen Street is the westernmost section of the ancient route that connected Colchester to its port at the Hythe on the river Colne to the east of the town. Once it would have been at the edge of town, as a medieval leper hospital had been sited there.[2] The route runs along the crest of a hill before descending to the waterfront, and enjoyed extensive views over the gardens and cornfields that lay behind the houses and over the river. By the mid-nineteenth century Magdalen Street mostly housed families who produced goods or services from home or went out to work, with only a handful of premises employing labour on site.

Cole's map of 1825 shows that the southern side of the street was more developed than the northern side, which was replete with market gardens and allotments, and shows no buildings to the west of Childwell Alley, on the northern side of the street.[3] Nineteenth-century photographs of Magdalen Street display an attractive and unpretentious collection of two-storey timber-framed and also newer brick houses and premises. The 1875 Ordnance Survey map shows the considerable infilling that had occurred since Cole's map was drawn, both along the street and behind it, creating yards and terraces at right angles to the main street. The plot of land enclosed between Magdalen Street and Childwell Alley – on Cole's 1825 map comprising two fields and some gardens – was, by 1875, crammed with buildings and courtyards. These houses were poorly constructed and of a lower standard than those in Magdalen Street, and few are still standing today. To the south a large estate of houses served by new roads had transformed the open fields into neat brick terraces with back gardens. A large number of varied businesses operated in Magdalen Street. There were second-hand shops, blacksmiths, bakers, carpenters and grocers, as well as accommodation for the 200–300 households listed in the 1851–81 censuses.

When Prince Albert's and the Duke of Cambridge's entourages arrived to inspect the camp they alighted at the town's main railway station to the north of the town.[4] But the soldiers routinely made use of the Hythe station on the Clacton line, which opened in 1849.[5] Troops regularly alighted at Hythe station and marched up Hythe Hill and along Magdalen Street to the garrison, accompanied by a mob of women. Reverend Olivier, who had clearly witnessed the spectacle, commented on 'the unmistakable character of those [girls] who accompany the soldiers as they march through the town'.[6] It is likely that these women were local girls, as the army would not have paid the train fares for camp followers. At one point in the second half of the nineteenth century they would have passed a total of 18 licensed premises as they marched the mile from the station to the camp.[7] Some of these premises – in particular, the Red Cross, the Yorkshire Grey, the Lifeboat, the Wellington, the Sawyer's Arms, the Colchester Arms and the Mariners, all in Magdalen Street – were named and shamed at annual licensing days for being associated with prostitution.[8] As we have already seen, Magdalen Street also housed brothels in Childwell Alley, Bretts Buildings and Barn Yard.

In 1830 the Beer Act was passed, which reduced magistrates' previous powers to control the alcohol licensing system. After 1830 the bench controlled the licences of public houses that sold spirits and beer, while the excise authority issued licences for a new type of drinking establishment, the beerhouse, which, as the name suggests, sold only beer. This new law enabled any rate-paying householder in England and Wales to brew and sell beer from their own house, provided they bought a two-guinea licence. The stated purpose of the law was to encourage the drinking of beer rather than spirits such as gin. Initially it may have been a new opportunity for entrepreneurial families to improve their prospects, but by the time the garrison arrived in Colchester in 1856 the town's brewers had successfully moved in to control most of the town's beerhouses. In 1869 the magistrates were given control of issuing licences for both public houses and beerhouses. Every autumn the bench held its licensing meeting, sometimes referred to as its brewster session, where landlords had to appear

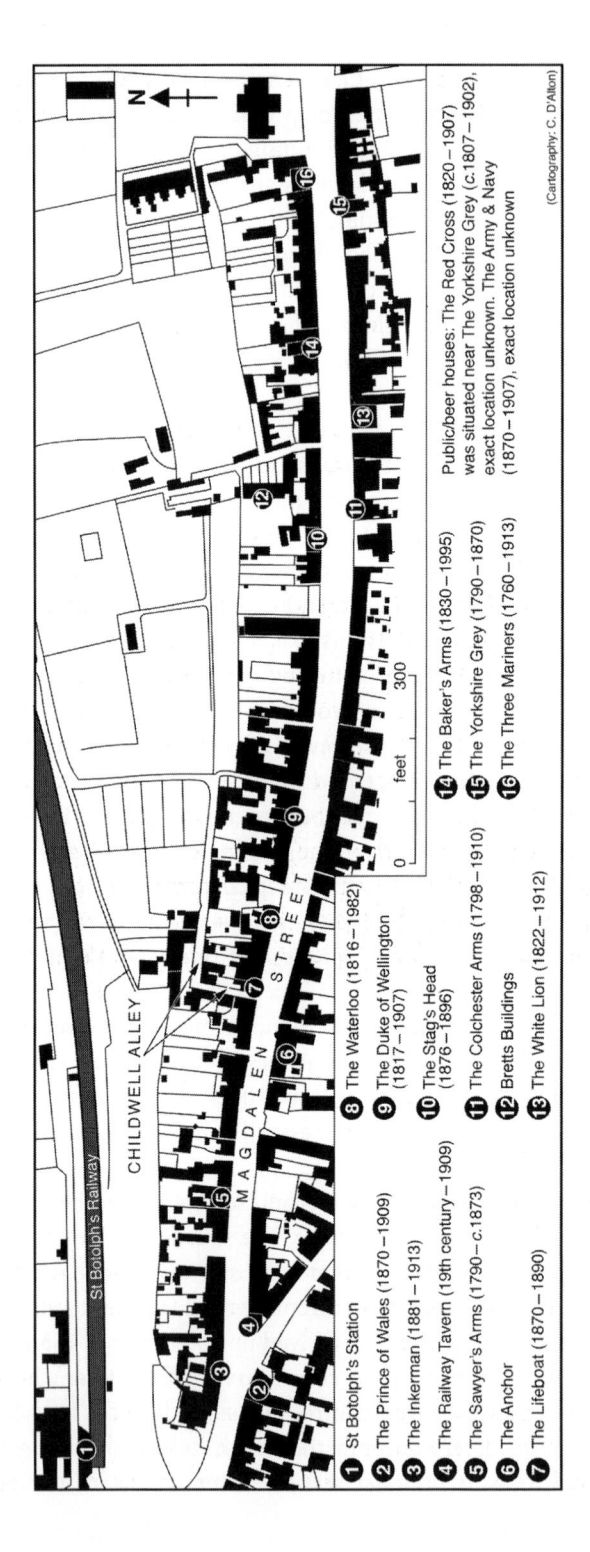

Figure 13. Map, showing Magdalen Street and the location of some of its many beer houses and brothels.

and (re)apply for their licences. The initial meeting was usually followed by several additional meetings where problematic licences were considered.

Colchester had a temperance society from 1837 that was re-established in 1854, suggesting that the original founders struggled to raise support. In addition, the Colchester Young Men's Temperance Association was set up in 1861 and met in the Temperance Hall in Osborne Street. Both these societies worked to reduce drinking by providing men with alternative entertainment and by petitioning to reduce public-house opening hours.

Beer may have been a healthier option than gin, but public drunkenness remained a significant problem. In 1857 the category 'drunk and disorderly and assaults' in the police returns accounted for 42 per cent of the previous year's charges, demonstrating one of the negative impacts that the new garrison was having on the town.[9] While police were expected to check out licensed premises on their beat, they were not expected to linger there. In the early years of the developing Victorian police force constables were frequently dismissed for being drunk on duty. The police did not arrest every drunk, preferring to encourage them to go home quietly, and prostitutes constituted only a small proportion of the men and women who regularly disturbed the peace in this way. Arrests of prostitutes for drunkenness were complicated by the expectation that pub and beerhouse landlords would exert some control over their presence and behaviour on licensed premises and that the police would be summoned only as a last resort. However, once the drunken prostitute left the beerhouse she became an uninhibited woman trying to find her way home along the public street, which was a less complicated situation for the constable to deal with. He would advise her to go home, even help her in the right direction, and only arrest her if she was aggressive or incapably drunk. Our database reveals that for every prostitute arrested on the premises at the Lifeboat and the Anchor two more were arrested for drunken disorder in Magdalen Street. This risk of being arrested in the street for drunkenness was one of the disadvantages involved in part-time prostitution and in living independently as a prostitute. The ensuing fine or prison sentence could disrupt an already difficult life.

The Lifeboat Inn was situated on the corner of Childwell Alley. Its nearest competitors were the Sawyer's Arms to the west and the Waterloo Inn to the east. It was owned by brewers Messrs Stewart, Pattison & Company, and was described as 'a substantially built brick and slated building, erected and specially adapted for a public house'.[10] In fact it never had a spirit licence, so was always a beerhouse. It was probably set up in the mid-1850s, but the first evidence for it appears in *Kelly's Directory* of 1862 and in a report that its landlord, George Butcher, was fined for selling gin there in 1863.[11] In the same year it was named as the site of a theft and, the following year, as a refuge for the men who assaulted prostitute Mary Ann Cosgrove.[12]

10 *ES* 27 August 1892.
11 *ES* 1 July 1863. The 1861 census named only one licensed premises – the Sawyer's Arms – although it listed seven beerhouse and innkeepers in Magdalen Street. At the 1892 brewster session solicitor Mr Jones claimed that the Lifeboat had been licensed for 50 years, while the agent for the owners claimed 40 years only.
12 *ES* 27 January and 20 April 1864.
13 *ES* 24 October 1891.
14 *ES* 26 January 1872.
15 *Chelmsford Chronicle* 8 January 1875.
16 However, a Harmer family, consisting of a mother Jessey, born in 1829, and her two daughters, tailoress Wilhelmina, aged 15, and Eliza, aged 11, lived in lodgings next door to the Lifeboat. The 1861 census shows that Jessey's eldest daughter was Sarah Ann, a tailoress born in Brightlingsea in 1843, so it is possible that Ann Harmer was connected to this family.
17 *ES* 5 May 1876.
18 *ES* 18 January and 13 December 1879.
19 *ES* 1 August 1885.
20 *IJ* 6 March 1880.
21 *ES* 27 August 1892.
22 *ES* 6 March 1886. The woman's name was Susannah Heath and she had been a patient in the lock hospital some years before.
23 *ES* 10 July 1886. In the event the licence was renewed after a caution.
24 *ES* 21 August 1886
25 *IJ* 19 October 1886.
26 *ES* 19 November 1892.
27 *IJ* 12 November 1886.
28 *ES* 2 September 1870.
29 *ES* 27 December 1890.
30 Jephcott, *The Inns, Taverns and Pubs of Colchester*, p. 25.
31 *ES* 21 August 1857.
32 *ES* 7 September 1859 and 22 June 1860.
33 *ES* 7 October 1870.
34 *ES* 2 February 1872.
35 *ES* 21 July 1876.
36 *ES* 15 September 1876.
37 *ES* 24 August 1878.

CHAPTER 6

The Contagious Diseases Acts and the lock hospital

Unhappily I was no stranger to the scandalous, pestiferous and miserable operation of these Acts.[1]

The second part of this book will consider how those with money and power in Colchester tried to deal with the problems that prostitution presented. The story revealed by our sources is complex and contested because those who might have made a contribution to suppressing the vice trade operated from competing perspectives and motives and were inclined to attempt to disguise any unacknowledged support of immorality. Legally there was room for a great deal of discretion and as a result the problem itself was not clearly identified. It was the anti-social and health implications of prostitution that were targeted, rather than the activity itself. Dealing with anti-social behaviour and venereal disease involved public expenditure and neighbourhood issues, and from time to time the newspaper reported small eruptions of disquiet and disgust that more was not done to acknowledge and deal with the problems. Most people did not go to such lengths to express their disapproval, but others were galvanised to try to avert the tide of immorality in more constructive ways, albeit small in scale.

Both syphilis and gonorrhea were included in the term venereal disease, having been distinguished in 1838 by a French physician, Philippe Ricord. The power of syphilis to cause epidemics in populations not previously affected is well known. In the eighteenth century, for instance, several towns in Norway suffered in this way.[2] By the mid-nineteenth century the prevalence of syphilis outbreaks among the general population had weakened, although the army, responsible for a good deal of its incidence (until penicillin was discovered to be a cure in the 1940s), continued to attempt to combat its ability to cause epidemics in barracks.[3] While the more unlucky patients passed directly from primary to secondary forms of the disease, suffering and dying from the symptoms of acute syphilis in a short period of time, most individuals survived the primary symptoms and lived for years before the disease reappeared in its final form. But unless the individual's immune system was very robust, both syphilis and gonorrhea caused chronic symptoms, could infect sexual partners and wore away the vital organs, eventually causing death.

The bacterium causing syphilis was identified in 1905 and the Wassermann test to identify its presence in the body was developed in 1906. When Colney Hatch Asylum in Middlesex first used the test in 1912 it was discovered that 10 per cent of its male patients were suffering from the symptoms of brain degeneration caused by tertiary syphilis.[4] Salvarsan, the first antibacterial (arsenic-based) drug used against syphilis, was marketed from 1909. The nineteenth-century medical profession understood the infectious and fluctuating nature of syphilis and employed a variety of treatments, such as calomel (mercurous chloride). Unfortunately this remedy had toxic side effects, including disabling dental and neurological symptoms. Some doctors experimented with new ideas such as inoculation and mercury administered through steam; others discussed ways of dealing with the side effects of mercury poisoning. Most practitioners put their trust in mercury applied orally or directly to a lesion, its poisonous effects reduced with sarsaparilla and chlorate of potash.[5]

As we saw in Chapter 1, a Royal Commission report of 1857 gave Colchester's garrison a poor record for venereal disease, and by 1862 almost half its servicemen had been affected. The 1857 report caused consternation in Colchester. The camp's military hospital treated venereal soldiers, but venereal women were the town's responsibility. At this date infectious patients were normally treated at home, the medical practitioner doing what he could to reduce cross infection in the family and neighbourhood. Only in cases of smallpox or cholera did the town authorities attempt to set up special isolation arrangements. It is unlikely that Colchester would have made any special arrangements for venereal women without pressure being exerted by the garrison. Using Treasury funding, Colchester's Board of Guardians set up a temporary foul ward (syphilis was known colloquially as the 'foul disease') in 1860 in a building at the back of its Union workhouse site. The Board's meeting minutes reveal that a letter written by the garrison's commanding officer offered financial assistance for the provision of an 'outhouse with a separate entrance' at the workhouse where the Union medical officer could treat venereal women.[6] Although this outhouse arrangement makes it sound as though the prostitutes were to be treated as moral outcasts too polluting to use the main entrance or infirmary ward at the workhouse, it is more likely that the

Guardians were anxious to placate the rate payers (who might have objected to money being spent in this way) and to emphasise the women's non-pauper status by providing them with a separate entrance into the workhouse.[7] The poor law was intended to support only the destitute and a working prostitute was not considered to be in this category.

Meanwhile, parliament was under pressure from the army to legislate to control prostitution. The first Contagious Diseases Act (CDA) was passed in 1864 in an attempt to reduce syphilis among soldiers and sailors. The act was passed at 2am with virtually no parliamentary or public debate by a secret armed forces committee using friendly witnesses.[8] Two further CDAs in 1866 and 1869 extended its scope. The CDAs empowered police to arrest prostitutes in selected ports or army towns such as Colchester and to compel them to undergo medical examinations at fortnightly intervals. If the lock hospital medical officer saw symptoms of venereal disease the woman was placed in a lock hospital until the symptoms disappeared, which might take several months. The police drew up lists of women they observed to be prostitutes and sometimes they overstepped the mark. *Reynold's Newspaper* reported an incident in Colchester in which a respectable domestic servant was observed talking to a friend who was on the list drawn up by the lock hospital police. Despite her claim that she was a respectable woman, she was swiftly compelled into the CDA system and had great difficulty extricating herself.[9] Most respectable women caught up in such circumstances refused to be medically examined and relied on a relative or employer to provide the necessary testimonial.[10]

The aim of the act was to protect men from infected women; it made no reference to protecting women from infected men. The rationale for imprisoning only women with the disease was based on cultural double standards and the current state of medical understanding about pathology and the female body, which included the idea, supported by *The Lancet*, that the prostitute was the conduit of venereal infection. As Finnegan explains, the myth of the natural sinfulness of women was a function of 'the middle-class Victorian male's ignorance, fear, prejudice and guilt'.[11] The army had its own ways of humiliating and punishing soldiers who were found to have venereal disease, including loss of pay and leave for soldiers hospitalised with venereal disease. Medical officers also organised what were colloquially known as 'dangle parades', in which soldiers drawn up in lines exposed their genitals for medical inspection. Next of kin were also sometimes informed if a soldier was diagnosed with venereal disease. Such punishments had the effect of reducing the incidence of cases reported and they were discontinued after 1910.[12] Army medical statistics show that venereal disease was a major cause of soldiers' hospitalisation at this time. Reducing this drain on manpower was the sole purpose of the CDAs.

6   ERO, G/Co M9, Guardian minutes for 29 May and 31 July 1860.
7   ERO, G/Co M9, 29 May 1860. The War Office contributed £50, only £10 of which was spent on providing the foul ward.
8   F.B. Smith, 'The Contagious Diseases Act Reconsidered', *Social History of Medicine*, 3 (1990) pp. 197–215.
9   The girl was recalled to the lock hospital having unwittingly signed a document there when first arrested, and spent a week there before being rescued into the local home for 'fallen' women. *Reynold's Newspaper* 20 November 1870.
10 The *Essex Standard* reported several incidents where respectable girls were arrested by mistake in Colchester, but the error was usually quickly reversed.
11 Finnegan, *Poverty and Prostitution*, p. 8.
12 H. Mayhew et al., *The London Underworld in the Victorian Period: Authentic First-person Accounts by Beggars, Thieves and Prostitutes* (Mineola, NY, 2005), pp. 41–3.
13 ERO, G/Co M9, 28 November 1865.
14 ERO, G/Co M9, 26 February 1861. Twenty years before, the Woodbridge Guardians had appointed 'a steady female to superintend the ward of the unchaste women in the House'. SRO, ADA 12/AB1/4. We are indebted to Angela Miller for this reference.
15 Lock hospitals originated as institutions to isolate leprosy patients and to prevent them from wandering about potentially infecting others.
16 J. Pearson and M. Rayner, 'Colchester's Lock Hospital, 1869–86', *Essex Journal*, 47/1 (2012), pp. 20–27.
17 *The Times* 21 July 1870.
18 In 1874 Edward Waylen, who was the brother of a Colchester magistrate, was appointed the town's first medical officer of health, a vote of confidence in a competitive professional world, suggesting that he was admired for the work he did on behalf of the War Office.
19 J.R. Lane, 'Notes on the Practice of the Female London Lock Hospital', *British Medical Journal*, 5 December 1868, p. 592.
20 Walkowitz, *Prostitution and Victorian Society*, p. 4.
21 *Ibid.*, p. 90.
22 Petrie, *A Singular Iniquity*, p. 105.
23 Some placards advertised Storks' suggestion that army wives should also be subject to medical examinations. Chesney, *The Victorian Underworld*.
24 Martin, *The Story of Colchester*, p. 102. A. Phillips, 'Four Colchester Elections: Voting Behaviour in a Victorian Market Town', in K. Neale (ed.), *An Essex Tribute: Essays Presented to Frederick G. Emmison as a Tribute to his Life and Work for Essex* (London, 1987), pp. 199–227.
25 *Essex and West Suffolk Gazette* 4 November 1870.
26 S.S. Holton, *Suffrage Days: Stories from the Women's Suffrage Movement* (London, 1996).
27 Phillips, 'Four Colchester Elections', pp. 199–227.
28 *Essex and West Suffolk Gazette* 4 February 1870.
29 *ES* 11 November 1870.
30 Trustram, *Women of the Regiment*; Skelley, *The Victorian Army at Home*.
31 A.V. John and C. Eustace, *The Men's Share? Masculinities, Male Support and Women's Suffrage in Britain, 1890–1920* (London, 1997), p. 7.
32 *ES* 18 November 1870.
33 *ES* 18 November 1870.
34 Brown, *Colchester*, p. 168.
35 HC/CL/JO/10: correspondence relating to the Colchester Lock Hospital, House of Commons Unprinted Papers Collection, 25 May 1871.
36 *ES* 20 November 1880.

37 *ES* 26 November 1881. When Josephine Butler came to Colchester for the 1870 election Mrs Marriage's house was her first port of call.
38 *ES* 12 April 1884.
39 *ES* 19 April and 24 April 1884.
40 *ES* 6 March 1886.
41 The *Essex Standard* reported the disbanding of the lock hospital police force; *ES* 19 May 1883.
42 ERO, Mf 223 G/Co M23–25.

31   *ES* 13 September 1884.
32   *ES* 10 September 1875.
33   *ES* 12 March 1875.
34   *ES* 8 July 1882.
35   *ES* 1 September 1865.
36   *ES* 3 September 1892 and 24 June 1893.
37   *ES* 20 September 1890.
38   *ES* 10 September 1869.
39   *ES* 16 December 1857. Both women received prison sentences, one with hard labour.
40   *ES* 10 September 1869. Three of the five licences were not renewed on this occasion.
41   'He undertook to get rid of the woman and turn the houses into warehouses if the Bench would allow the case to drop on payment of costs.' *ES* 7 February 1889.
42   *ES* 27 October 1888. The 'girl' under discussion was Emma Middleton.
43   Petrie, *A Singular Iniquity*, p. 103.
44   *ES* 5 March 1892.
45   *ES* 7 May 1875.
46   *ES* 18 October 1867.
47   *ES* 13 September 1890.
48   *ES* 6 August 1892. The boy survived and is to be found in the 1911 census living in a caravan.

CHAPTER 8

The role of Colchester's solicitors

Mr TABOR (rising). Are you interfering to teach me?
Mr JONES. I am addressing the Magistrate on behalf of my clients.
Mr TABOR. You were attempting to teach.
Mr JONES. Well, I hope none of us are too old
to learn something from one another.[1]

Christian's *Short History of Solicitors* makes the point that, by the last decade of the nineteenth century, every aspect of the solicitor's professional life – 'his education, his right to practice, his relations with his employers, his remuneration' – was subject to regulations laid down by parliament. By this date those entering the profession were required to sit examinations and be articled for five years (unless they were graduates, in which case articles were for three years). Barristers, unlike solicitors, were educated at university and acted as advocates in cases brought to them by solicitors. Christian remarks that, as a result, 'the attorney who knew the case thoroughly was not allowed to plead it; the man who could be heard sometimes did not read his brief.'[2] The County Courts Act of 1846 allowed solicitors to act as advocates in county courts and police courts, but barristers continued their monopoly of superior courts throughout the nineteenth century. Police inspectors and accountants could also present cases in court and judges could refuse to allow solicitors to plead. The *Essex Standard* quoted an article from the *Law Times* in which a Colchester solicitor defending two men before Colchester county court was told he had no right to be there. The reason given was that the solicitor 'knew a remand was to be asked for and therefore had no right to appear'. The editor, unable to accept such reasoning, quoted the law, which recognised 'the right of advocates to appear in all cases in which a summary conviction may follow'.[3] This is a local example of a response to developments in the legal profession.

The Law Society set up the register of solicitors in 1843, 15 years before the medical profession set up the General Medical Council to register its own approved practitioners.

Throughout the nineteenth century the legal profession, like the medical profession, learnt how to distance itself from untrained practitioners, how to co-operate so as to protect its own interests as a profession and how to exert power over clients. The solicitor's duties covered three main areas – giving business advice and preparing contracts, acting as a legal agent for litigants and preparing property conveyancing documentation. In order to make a living the solicitor employed clerks to orchestrate the more menial tasks, allowing him to concentrate on building up the business.[4] The increasing power of the police to take over the role of public prosecutor was an annoyance to some solicitors, who 'expressed their concerns in terms of class'.[5] Solicitors were socially inferior to barristers, judges and magistrates and, as Joanne McEntee points out in relation to Irish property exchanges, this branch of the profession was 'viewed with some disdain by members of the landed gentry'. She claims that in England the profession became more respectable by the end of the century as their clientele became increasingly socially diverse.[6]

This professional development can clearly be seen in the annals of Colchester borough, where solicitors worked in every court – police courts, Petty and Quarter Sessions – all of which dealt with minor crimes and anti-social behaviour, and also in the county court, which was set up in 1846 to deal with civil cases such as debt, bankruptcy and business conflicts. Each of these courts was under the jurisdiction of the bench of magistrates, all of whom had considerable social status as gentlemen, businessmen or doctors. The solicitors, by contrast, tended to have emerged from less well-connected families. Henry Jones (1826–89), 'son of a Waterloo hero', began as a mere shop boy aged 15.[7] Asher Prior, born 1850, was a confectioner's son. Both men were born in Colchester and their families were interconnected. Mr Jones was articled to Colchester solicitor F.G. Abell and taken into partnership, and then married Miss Ada Abell. Through his sister's marriage to a confectioner, Mr Jones was Asher Prior's uncle.

Unlike some members of the medical profession in Colchester, who practised for a few years before abandoning their calling for some other academic or political activity, Colchester's nineteenth-century solicitors seem to have achieved social progression through their business. They did this by taking on additional salaried roles such as town clerk, coroner, superintendent registrar of births, deaths and marriages, clerk to the Union Board of Guardians, notary public and so on. Asher Prior, like most of his legal colleagues, including Mr Jones and Mr Goody, was a town councillor and clearly made his mark early, aged 27. He was rebuked in a council meeting for time wasting with the put-down 'if anything could teach Mr Asher Prior modesty it would be this humbling reproof'.[8] The town's leading solicitors were heavily involved in a variety of municipal schemes for town improvement and used their insider knowledge to their political group's advantage. Andrew Phillips draws attention to the involvement of Henry Jones and Henry Goody in the town's Gas Company debacle, where 'that fine dividing line between public good and private profit' was called into question; Mr Goody was the Gas Company's solicitor, while Mr Jones attacked the Company's Gas Amendment bill of 1875.[9] In addition, several solicitors became successful businessmen in a private capacity, buying and developing property, brickyards and hotels. In the context of Colchester's vice trade some solicitors were involved in prosecuting and defending prostitutes, brothel keepers and their customers in court and some were also heavily involved, usually as advocates for brewers but occasionally in their own interest, in the annual brewster meetings, where public house licences were under discussion. By contrast, Asher Prior was active in temperance societies that favoured reducing this trade.[10] At least two solicitors owned property that was used for prostitution.

In the majority of the court cases involving prostitutes the police brought and proved the case before the bench in Petty and Quarter Sessions without any assistance from local solicitors, relying on the town clerk (who was a solicitor) to provide any legal direction they needed. Clive Emsley makes the point that by the mid-nineteenth century

> most criminal prosecutions in England were brought by private individuals ... [who] had to pay for the preparation of an indictment as well as any other expenses incurred by themselves, by their witnesses and by any counsel they employed ... . In some areas the new police appear to have taken over the role of public prosecutors from their inception, mainly for the many 'victimless' offences like drunkenness, but also when the victims were poor or female.[11]

Around 30 (9 per cent) of the women in our database were recorded by a newspaper having interactions with a solicitor in court, the cases split approximately equally between defence and prosecution. Some of the women were also indirectly affected, perhaps called as a witness when a solicitor proceeded with a brothel clearance case. Occasionally an association such as the NSPCC, the Colchester Licensed Victuallers' Association or a society for the prosecution of felons engaged a solicitor's services as prosecutor. About a third of Colchester's solicitors were identified by the newspaper defending or prosecuting cases involving prostitutes, although almost all of them were concerned with only one or two prostitute cases during the whole period. The three solicitors most frequently recorded in this connection were Henry Jones, Henry Goody and Asher Prior.

Figure 18. Mr Henry Jones, solicitor, whose canny understanding of people and business enabled him to rise from humble origins to become a man of property and influence in Colchester.

Henry Jones' practice was, according to the newspaper reports, the one most involved in these cases throughout the period 1857–1900.[12] He was born in Colchester in 1826 and, after training as a clerk and then being articled in two local firms, he set up on his own in Butt Road in 1854. He later moved his office to West Stockwell Street, where his clerks' windows overlooked a brothel. Two of his sons entered the law, one as a barrister and the other in his father's practice from the 1880s. Mr Jones is reported as defending just five of the women in our database. The fees for most of these cases were paid by those with an interest, such as the parish clergyman or the brothel keeper. The clergyman had a duty to bring brothels in his parish to public attention, spending parish rates money to do so as necessary. The brothel keeper sometimes engaged a solicitor to fight his case and paid for the privilege. Mr Jones' first case, in his third year in practice, concerned two prostitutes, one of them a married woman, charged with being drunk and disorderly. Both were given a month's hard labour. Then a girl called Ellen Day twice used his services, the first time when charged with stealing some pieces of meat from a pork butcher and the second time when accused of shoplifting a jar of pomatum from a chemist's in Head Street. In the first case the prosecutor decided not to press charges and in the second case Mr Jones successfully argued there was no evidence of a felony.[13] He also defended Emma Saunders, who was accused of assaulting another woman, by proving 'great provocation', which persuaded the bench to dismiss the case.[14]

Only with the fifth prostitute case that he defended was Mr Jones obliged to exert himself to earn his fee. In 1867 Private Ringrose Devereux accused prostitute Jane Mighton and another soldier, John Brown, of stealing his purse, which, thanks to a legacy, contained £23, a sum representing about a year's pay for a soldier of his rank. Jane said Devereux had given his purse to her and they had spent the money on a day out. In fact, when the prisoners were picked up three days after the spree a new silver watch was found on John Brown and 'a new dress piece, a new brooch, the prosecutor's purse' were among items found on Jane Mighton, the implication being that the items were bought with Devereux's legacy.[15] Mr Goody, prosecuting, described the events of the day, which involved a lengthy pub crawl including an expedition by hired pony and trap from Colchester to Lexden. Mr Jones, who liked to lull the bench and the prosecuting counsel by exploring the contingent details at length before exposing the fault in the evidence that would sway the case in his client's favour, asked Devereux many questions before complaining that his voice was inaudible.

Mr Jones having several times requested the prosecutor to speak out without much apparent effect, the Mayor said – Speak out, as if you were drilling a company of soldiers.

Figure 19. A view of Lexden, a village west of Colchester, then a popular destination for a Sunday afternoon stroll.

Mr Goody said the witness had been suffering so severely that he had only just left hospital, which might account for his speaking so low.

Mr Jones – But he speaks out sometimes.

Mr Hawkins [magistrate] – Perhaps that is an exertion.

[Devereux] to Mr Jones – If I had you in a company I could drill you (laughter).

Mr Jones – He says, sir, that if he had me in a company of soldiers he would give me 'what for' (laughter).

Mr Hawkins – He said he could drill you.

Mr Jones – Perhaps I could return the compliment and drill him.

Mr Goody – I think you are drilling him enough (renewed laughter).

No doubt this knock-about routine put Devereux off his guard and he went on to confess that he knew Jane Mighton well, had given her money at various times, sometimes every night; 'in fact he had kept her the last nine or ten months'. After that it was easy for Mr Jones to submit that 'there was no case on which a jury could convict'. Devereux's story had changed before their eyes and he had also admitted to being too drunk to know what had gone on at Lexden. In his summing up 'at some length Mr Jones entered into the connexion between the female prisoner and the prosecutor, she being sufficiently respectable, he might term it, to live under his protection for 9 or 10 months' before the mayor 'intimated that Mr Jones need not address them further upon the subject'. The bench did not refer the case to trial but discharged the prisoners with a warning.[16]

What message did such a report convey to the *Essex Standard*'s readership? Mr Jones had made cohabitation sound respectable in the context of prostitution and he had laid the blame for the serious crime firmly on Private Devereux, the victim, who had allowed himself to get incapably drunk while in possession of a considerable sum of money. The question of where the remainder of the money had gone was not raised and the unedifying details were obscured by the sheer exuberance of Mr Jones' clever presentation.

In seven cases, involving nine of the prostitutes recorded in our database, Mr Jones was prosecuting counsel, but his contribution in court is not described in detail. In five of these cases a prostitute was charged. Two of the women had their cases dismissed, three paid fines and one received a jail sentence, while the outcome for the seventh is not known. The remaining cases involved prostitutes as witnesses or victims of attack. Whether prosecuting or defending, Mr Jones could be relied upon to argue his case with flair and humour and the newspaper often quoted him at length and gave the bench's response, which might be querulous or dignified. In this way the activities of a few prostitutes and their clients were given some public attention and either or both sometimes became figures of fun rather than deplorable examples of anti-social behaviour.

Mr Jones also defended men caught up in the vice trade. Early in his career, in 1856 and 1857, he defended three such men. The first two were James Brittee, landlord of the Bath Hotel (whom the magistrates acquitted), and William Minter, landlord of the Clarence in Trinity Street: both were accused of harbouring prostitutes. In the latter case he persuaded the bench to drop the case and allow time for a replacement landlord to be found. The third was the case of William Tyler, landlord of a beerhouse on St John's Green, who was accused of serving gin without a spirit licence. An excise officer had visited the beerhouse and treated a prostitute, Susannah Hutton, to a glass of ale. While there he noticed the landlady serving Susannah a glass of gin and the landlord, who had not been present, was charged. After some preliminary jousting Mr Jones called William Tyler's daughter and his prostitute lodger to give evidence and he claimed that no excise visit had been anticipated and that no gin had been disposed of (in other words, poured away to escape detection) on the night. An adjournment was agreed so that the origin of the gin could be sought but two days later two magistrates reconvened to decide the case and 'gave the defendant the benefit of the doubt and dismissed the information'.[17]

These three cases occurred just as the garrison arrived in Colchester and Mr Jones demonstrated a wily approach when defending the morally suspect provision of premises from which prostitutes could ply their trade. Initially his skill lay in his ability to present the magistrates with what they wanted to hear – deferential platitudes, sophistry and casuistical arguments. However, once he had a little experience to fall back on, Mr Jones began to use his position to challenge the bench's complacency and the methods used by the police. Although the challenge was often reported as an unexpected intervention, in fact close reading reveals that Mr Jones was a man in control of his game. In 1861 he came to court for the case of a soldier charged with robbing a young woman with violence, a case that had been remanded twice before as the evidence was contradictory and incomplete. It was not an auspicious start, as no magistrates appeared; they had to be sent for and the court business was delayed by nearly an hour. Mr Jones, who must have known the odds were against his client, made a formal objection to the head constable's deposition, which had reported some casual conversation between the prisoner, the head constable and the magistrates. He was reported to have said:

> it was not in the power either of the police, the Magistrate, nor even the Lord Chief Justice, to interrogate a prisoner, and that it was repugnant to every principle of our constitution: and he protested against the evidence in question being allowed to remain upon the depositions.

The magistrates agreed to relinquish the questionable part of the statement and Mr Jones was then free to make his case for the defence.[18]

Most of Colchester's prostitutes seem to have depended on the police to present their case, whether they were complainant or defendant. But Mr Jones also took on some of the brothel-clearance cases, all of which involved prostitutes as witnesses, and he defended some men charged with a prostitute-related misdemeanour. Again, he often tried to reduce the impact of the crime. For instance, Mr Jones defended William Platford's application to take on the licence for the Wellington Inn in Magdalen Street, which the police had persuaded the bench to refuse on the grounds that Platford 'was not a man likely to conduct the house properly'. Mr Jones went above the police, not only making claims for Platford's 'excellent character' but also trying to shame the bench.

> For a period of 12 or 14 years he was in close and intimate employment with the late Alderman Wolton and he should like to know what Mr Wolton would have thought if he had occupied the Chair and heard the chief of police say that Platford was not a fit person to receive a license for carrying on business at a public house.[19]

In fact William Platford had a history of running poorly conducted premises in the previous decade but Mr Jones' tactic of appealing to the collegiate instincts of the bench was successful. At other times he used quite the opposite tactic, pitting one magistrate's opinion against another's.

In 1871 he defended Mr and Mrs Firmin, who had been charged with keeping a house of ill fame in Pelham's Lane off the High Street. This case involved some exchanges of bad temper in court, engineered by Mr Jones, who evidently decided that attack was the best means of defence in this case. He complained bitterly about the conditions under which the Firmins had been held. He spoke of the 'animosity and vindictiveness' of witnesses and accused the bench of wrongly demanding costs from the defendants which the parish should have paid. John Richer, the landlord of the Queen's Arms in Pelham's Lane, turned out to be the chief witness, and had to refute Mr Jones's accusation that he was motivated by malice. The Metropolitan police inspector in charge of the lock hospital testified to seeing prostitutes in both the Queen's Arms and Firmin's house, and repeated Firmin's comment that 'these girls must go somewhere and they may as well come to my house as go anywhere else'. Mr Jones recommended that the bench allow the matter to drop, implying that the Firmins would not dare to offend in this way again. The bench, evidently offended by his abrasive style, declined his advice and referred the case to Quarter Sessions. Mr Jones then demanded it go instead to the Assizes and an argument followed as to whether bail was adequate, with the senior magistrate, Mr Tabor, becoming seriously annoyed by Mr Jones' presumption. He protested angrily that Jones was 'interfering to teach me … . I don't think it is for one in your position to teach me.' Mr Jones did not apologise until after he had won his point at the Assizes several months later.[20] This case is a good example of the difficulties involved in brothel-clearance cases before the law was changed in 1885. It is not surprising that parish vestries were unwilling to take a brothel owner to court and incur heavy expenditure to see their case challenged by a clever solicitor and responsibility evaded by empty promises.

In 1886, when brothers George and William Last were accused of allowing a brothel in Bretts Buildings in Magdalen Street, Mr Jones defended them. This was the first case in Colchester under the 1885 Criminal Law Amendment Act. He successfully argued that the Lasts, who ran a bakery, were ignorant of 'the class of people who occupied the houses and of what took place there'. The bench dismissed the case against the elder brother, while the younger brother escaped with the payment of costs and a relatively small fine.[21] Mr Jones, like his colleague Mr Goody, might question the methods of both police and magistrates in court, sometimes being confrontational and sometimes obfuscating. His eloquence and wit were clearly enjoyed, even if he did not win the day.[22] None of his work, as reported in the *Essex Standard*, suggests he had patronising attitudes to the prostitutes who came his way as clients and witnesses.[23]

Mr Jones was also very active on annual licensing days representing the interests of several brewers and becoming more skilled year by year at maximising loopholes in the law for his brewer clients' benefit. In 1865, for instance, he proposed every one of the applications for new licences, ten in all, four of which were granted. The following year he asked for a licence for his own property – the Langham Hotel, which he had had built in the High Street. The discussion revealed the politics of the bench, with the conservative William Waylen, a retired doctor, trying to muzzle the liberal James Tabor, who wanted to oppose the application with facts and figures relating population numbers to licensed premises numbers. The licence was granted. Two years later Mr Jones bought the Sir Colin Campbell, a disreputable pub in the Mersea Road near the Camp. At first he tried to distance himself from the suspect business by telling the bench, 'although the person now living there never has been a tenant of mine, I own the property which I let to a firm of brewers'.[24] Not being granted a spirit licence, Mr Jones tried another tack by deciding not to let the two houses – no doubt brothels – adjoining his beerhouse.[25] Still this did not secure the licence, so he closed the house for a year and rethought the project as follows. He

> purchased the whole of the property at the back of the house and he was now laying out a new street which was being built upon and he thought anyone who went and looked at the locality would say he was effecting a very great public improvement ... he was endeavouring to arrange with the authorities for the closing of the narrow passageway by the side of the camp and diverting all the traffic into the intended new street which he

During the period of this study Colchester was home to around two dozen practising solicitors, a few of whom dealt with vice cases in the borough courts. Several of them were also deeply engaged in local politics and business in addition to their legal caseload. According to the *Standard*'s reports, Mr Jones and his son together dealt with at least 30 cases involving prostitutes and brothels, Mr Prior, Mr Goody and Mr Abell with less than a dozen apiece. In the context of their daily professional life such cases would not have been challenging. Nevertheless, it is clear that they accorded prostitute and brothel cases the same attention to detail as other cases, asking for adjournments when they had not had time to gather the necessary facts. In arguing for a prostitute accused of a crime they sought to reduce the significance of her disreputable lifestyle and/or to draw attention to the lack of credibility of her accuser's evidence.

A second and much more significant set of clients were the town's brewers and public-house owners, who could expand their business in the town only by increasing the numbers of premises where beer and spirits were sold. Every autumn licences came up for review and solicitors were employed in a head-to-head struggle to represent their own clients' applications and to try and defeat opposing applications. Before the garrison arrived this was a straightforward activity that did not take up much court time. But after the arrival of the garrison, when the number of beerhouses greatly increased, the licensing procedure became much more contested and the bench's decisions came under closer scrutiny. When applying for a new licence or protesting against a colleague's application on behalf of a client, the solicitors initially worked as competing individuals, but within ten years of the garrison's arrival they had begun to work together against the bench, a tactic the magistrates found difficult to deal with. Politics and self-interest were implicated in some spats, although this was rarely explicitly exposed by the newspaper.

During the 1840s and 1850s solicitors and medics set up the bodies that licensed and controlled their respective professions and individuals locally exerted pressure to bring their colleagues into line with the new rules and regulations. One of the effects of this was that both professions had to learn how to co-operate rather than to compete for their paying clientele. Colchester's borough courts were an arena where professional men met and exerted power. However, in trying to deal decisively with the effects of prostitution, professional confrontation was not helpful. Some solicitors had private business interests that engaged with suspect lodgings and beerhouses; professionally they had brewers, brothel keepers and prostitutes as clients. Their words as reported in the newspaper were sharp and to the point. Those magistrates who were doctors seem not to have engaged in such businesses but, in using the bench to raise their profile and social status, they also acquired a more gentlemanly and euphemistic turn of phrase. Some of the town's solicitors

THE ROLE OF COLCHESTER'S SOLICITORS

– Mr Jones in particular – confronted and exploited this characteristic with displays of aggression and humour that made for some lively exchanges and which the newspaper reported and sometimes highlighted in an editorial.

Notes

1. *ES* 13 October 1871.
2. E.B.V. Christian, *A Short History of Solicitors* (London, 1896), p. 211.
3. *ES* 11 February 1876.
4. Christian, *A Short History*.
5. Emsley, *The Great British Bobby*, p. 73.
6. J. McEntee, '"Gentleman Practisers": Solicitors as Elites in Mid-nineteenth Century Irish Landed society' (Academia edu, 2014).
7. Phillips, *Ten Men and Colchester*, p. 4.
8. *ES* 5 October 1877.
9. Phillips, *Ten Men and Colchester*, pp. 62–8.
10. Prior represented the Order of Good Templars at the 1875 brewster session to oppose the grant of any new licence and in 1877 occupied the chair in a meeting of the UK Alliance for the Total Suppression of the Liquor Traffic. *ES* 27 August 1875 and 16 February 1877.
11. Emsley, *The Great British Bobby*, p. 73.
12. Mr Jones died in 1889 aged 63, having served three years as town clerk 1877–80. His son, H.W. Jones, succeeded to the practice.
13. *ES* 10 April 1863 and 15 June 1864.
14. *ES* 22 May 1863.
15. *ES* 3 May 1867.
16. *ES* 8 May 1867.
17. *ES* 14 and 16 October 1857.
18. *ES* 26 April 1861. The magistrates consulted and decided to send the case to Quarter Sessions, meanwhile seeing 'no reason to reflect upon the conduct of the head constable'. At the Sessions the soldier was undefended and reliant on his own wits, which were insufficient to protect him. The jury found him guilty and he was given four years' penal servitude. *ES* 3 July 1861.
19. *ES* 23 February 1877.
20. See the quotation that heads this chapter which continued the argument. *ES* 13 October and 15 December 1871.
21. *ES* 28 August 1886.
22. He 'added to a pugnacious temperament a sharp mind and the ability to talk himself out of almost any situation'. Phillips, *Ten Men and Colchester*, p. 65.
23. When solicitor Mr Philbrick's son found a young vagrant, Rose Williams, sleeping in his plantation in broad daylight he gave her into custody. *ES* 2 March 1860.
24. *ES* 20 September 1867.
25. The annual licensing meeting in 1867 heard evidence from a soldier lodger that 'the third house from the Sir Colin Campbell was a very bad place and he had seen women from that house round various public houses in the town'. *ES* 2 October 1867.
26. *ES* 28 August 1868.
27. ES 21 January 1892. The case concerned Alice Dines of Magdalen Street.
28. Fisher, *Prostitution and the Victorians*.

CHAPTER 9

Adjudicating prostitution

Prisoner on being asked if she had anything to say ... said I hope you'll always have good shoes and never have to go barefoot or desolate.[1]

In 2013 Sir James Munby, President of the Family Division of the High Court, was reported as speaking about the need for modern judges to serve all faiths. He said Victorian judges were expected to promote virtue and discourage vice with 'a very narrow view of sexual morality'. He observed that at the time the Christian church also had a dominant influence.[2] In this chapter we will explore whether the attitude of the magistrates in Colchester to the explosion of immorality that took place after the arrival of the garrison in 1856 was indeed narrow. Chapter 11 will consider the church's approach.

The role of the magistrates
The 1835 Municipal Corporations Act continued to support the borough courts and Petty Sessions as before, and a new county court to deal with pleas of debt was added in 1846.[3] So for the second half of the nineteenth century Colchester's magistrates met in Petty Sessions, later renamed police courts, and the county court at least twice a month, and at borough Sessions quarterly. In addition, the annual licensing decisions often continued over several meetings from August to October before the business was completed. The mayor chaired the bench, his deputy taking over on the rare occasions he was absent. The town clerk, one of the town's solicitors appointed by the town council, was also in attendance, interposing from time to time with a point of law or an opinion. The bench heard cases presented by a borough police officer or, where the funds allowed, by solicitors for the defence and prosecution, who were a small

number of long-serving local attorneys. Most of the crimes they considered were decidedly petty by modern standards. Men and boys outnumbered women in the parade of delinquency, but several dozen women were caught each year, mostly for theft, drunken disorder and assault. A small proportion of these women were identified as 'unfortunates'.

Around 55 men served as borough magistrates in Colchester during the period 1850–1900. The majority were professionals and businessmen in the town, some still actively engaged and others retired. Very few had any legal training and they relied on the town clerk to provide legal guidance. The *Victoria County History* notes that the number of professionals in Colchester was relatively small, with 32 clergy, 28 medical men and 34 solicitors and lawyers resident in 1851, but that their influence economically, socially and politically was very great.[4] The clergy were prominent on the bench in other parts of Essex, but not in Colchester. The average number of years served was ten, but five magistrates, such as Major Bishop and Dr Williams, served more than 20 years. During this time one magistrate was removed from office.[5] In theory, the bench was usually a sufficiently large team to ensure that at least two or three magistrates would turn up on court days but, because there was no clear rota, numbers and continuity were not guaranteed.[6] The magistrates who remanded a case might well not be present when it came up again a few days later, meaning that relevant information might be forgotten between hearings. In earlier chapters we have noted magistrates being taken to task by solicitors, who became adept at exploiting this and other weaknesses in the court system. The magistrates were careful to maintain their own dignity and authority at all costs. To this end they were sure to support the police, to admonish bumptious solicitors and to withdraw to discuss a case or to delay a decision if it was contentious or if they were likely to disagree. The language they used was carefully chosen to be authoritative, consensual and dignified, sometimes to the detriment of clarity.

The magistrates worked in courts that admitted the public and the reports of the proceedings show that they were expected to respond to individuals, often clergymen, who came to court to raise particular concerns such as prostitution. Newspaper reporters also intervened on occasion, passing notes to the solicitors to correct the facts,[7] although they were not allowed to communicate with the bench. In 1858 an attempt by the police to restrict entry to 'respectable people' earned a rebuke from the *Essex Standard*.[8] So, although the courts were formal proceedings, there was also an informal and unplanned element. The report of the initial hearing of a gruesome murder case in 1891 gave a description of this public scrutiny and the bench's attempts to exercise control:

> That portion directly in front of the dock was set aside for witnesses and others engaged in the case … the gallery presented a sight not easily to be forgotten. Although the sterner

sex predominated on the whole, yet the gallery was chiefly occupied by females and as a judgment for their curiosity they were doomed to listen to cases both revolting and uninteresting before the one they had flocked to hear came on ... and although the Mayor suggested females should leave the court, only a few who had any respect for themselves did so, and those who did not must have been shocked by the evidence adduced ... .[9]

In 1885 the chairman of the Ipswich bench decided to make a statement about the implications of the new Criminal Law Amendment Act, which dealt with the closure of brothels and the raised age of consent, adding that 'it was a revolting and disagreeable subject to name from the bench, but he thought it his duty' to make those remarks in the presence of the public and the press'.[10]

In law in the period up to 1885 there were three approaches the bench could use to reduce prostitution: they could find prostitutes guilty of anti-social behaviour and send them to jail for short periods, they could refuse licences to pubs and beerhouses where prostitution occurred and they could close brothels brought to their attention by any of the town's parish officers. In earlier chapters we have explained why brothel closure by the authorities was a rare event before 1885. The first two approaches also failed initially, with the result that the problem developed to proportions that could not be ignored. The magistrates were obliged to find ways to obscure their lack of action and effectiveness. One strategy was to make moral judgements in court, which were respectfully recorded by the newspaper. When Elizabeth Dowsett and Caroline Ham misbehaved in 1857 the mayor proclaimed 'that the conviction of these two girls would have the effect of putting a stop to the riotous behaviour hitherto witnessed in Mersea Road'.[11] The bench described a married man who seduced a 14-year-old in the Colchester Arms in Magdalen Street as 'a disgrace to the married state', but accepted the landlady's denial that she knew either of the parties.[12]

The language used by the bench to deplore vice was generally more temperate than that used by the town's clergy and police. This was perhaps a reflection of eighteenth-century attitudes around keeping the peace, when magistrates had no police force to back them up and were compelled to consider the likely response, such as rioting, if they exerted their authority unjustly. The magistrates' statements on immorality were double-edged: on the one hand uncompromising and on the other unspecific. We have already quoted examples where the bench deplored the activities of a pub landlord and then proceeded to renew his licence.

The magistrates reserved their harshest language not for the prostitutes but for the individuals organising the trade in prostitution. Such people did not often come into court because they were more skilled than the prostitutes at evading the law and, in their case, the law was relatively easy to evade. But in 1858 the law caught up with Phoebe Ford, who kept a house of ill fame in

Priory Street. The mother of one of her harboured girls tried to rescue her daughter from the brothel and was assaulted by the 'very flashily dressed' Ford. The magistrates sided wholeheartedly with the mother, whose courage in bringing the case to court, they asserted, proved that she told the truth. The mayor continued in his best judgemental style:

> This was one of the most disgusting cases they had ever had before them, for there was no doubt that defendant kept a house for purposes the most vile, and he should not be doing his duty by her and others without telling her that at a certain day she would have to account for this. She not only sinned herself but pandered to the vice of others and was helping these poor girls towards Hell. She might smile but she would find that with every girl she was thus taking into her house she was not only assisting in their destruction but her own. He would do his utmost to cause her house to be indicted at the session.[13]

Almost none of the prostitutes, assuming the newspaper reports were reliable, were subjected to this kind of language.[14] This suggests that the magistrates were more tolerant of the prostitutes than they were of those who profited from their degradation. The euphemism 'unfortunate' was commonly chosen by the newspaper to describe the prostitutes involved, and the effect of this is perhaps to negate the idea that the women were responsible for their actions.

Another strategy was for some of the magistrates to be seen out and about patrolling the streets at night as if their very presence might quell vice. In June 1857 the mayor challenged solicitor Mr Goody to explain a comment he had made to the effect that

> some magistrate high in authority had been seen about the town at a late hour of the night watching private houses ... . Mr Goody said 'he had understood that a magistrate had been known to watch proceedings in the streets as late as 12 or 1 o'clock of a night. He said that he did not approve of that sort of thing and he did not think it maintained the dignity of the office.' He named the Mayor. He also disapproved of plain clothes police sent to entrap publicans into serving out of hours.

Clearly Mr Goody was speaking on behalf of publicans rather than their customers. The mayor rebuked him, saying 'I shall do so without asking the permission of any solicitor whatever', and Mr Goody apologised, tongue in cheek, claiming that he was only worried about 'whether it was a dignified way' to behave.[15] This must have been an awkward exchange for the mayor, caught between zeal and dignity in his public office and the suspicion that his actions were being denigrated by a mere attorney.

Knowledge gained in this way was used to support decisions that merely moved the problem on rather than dealing with it in a decisive way. The individuals accused of running disorderly premises – and their solicitors – often cited 'bad locality' as a reason for poor standards, an excuse with which the magistrates usually agreed: 'the Bench would consider that from a public house of a low description in a low neighbourhood it was next to impossible that characters of this sort could at all times be excluded, however vigilant the landlord might be'.[16] They accepted previous good character references and the stated wish of the publican to work in a better area. Some of this relaxed approach was to do with avoiding the retribution of the mob if too many of the poor man's pleasures were removed by his social superiors. One annual licensing meeting even gave the opinion that public houses were 'necessary evils, as everybody would allow'.[17] In addition, the bench could instruct the town's police to act in particular ways. In 1854, in the case of Thomas Platford's activities in living 'solely on the prostitution of women residing at his house', the mayor simply drew the bad reputation of Platford (and others) to the attention of the police with a view to 'suppressing the evil'. They suggested that police officers should be positioned where they could warn all comers that they were about to enter a den of thieves.[18] This threat was aimed at the pimps and the brothel customers rather than the prostitutes they harboured, and had little effect.

It could also be argued that the magistrates were hamstrung by rectitude in dealing with immorality in public, being reluctant to draw attention to disreputable subjects. In 1871 the borough Quarter Sessions dealt with a rare case centred on a house of ill fame in Stanwell Street (see Chapter 4). The husband and wife were charged together and, in a manner unlike the magistrates' usual procedure, the Recorder went to great lengths to explore the legal setting of such a case. In the presence of five magistrates and six barristers he explained that this wife could not be assumed to be her husband's legal responsibility: 'because this was a misdemeanour not a felony and the wife must have participated, this presumption does not apply'. He went on to remind them of a law passed under George II to put down nuisances of this kind which allowed magistrates to commit to trial offenders who had been reported by a police constable and two rate-paying neighbours willing to prosecute. He set out the right of the police to bring such a charge. Both prosecution and defence were in agreement that airing the facts would be a mistake, the former on grounds of public decency and the latter on the grounds that 'the prisoners had pleaded guilty on the faith of the arrangement come to before the Magistrates, and they would therefore be placed in a wrong position'. The Recorder would have none of this, which is what makes the case unusual. He said he was anxious 'to ascertain whether or not there had been a public nuisance as well as a private one'. Since this was a case of 'public nuisance which had caused a great scandal', he said some information was necessary. At the very least he wanted to know 'how long the house had been kept and to what extent the law had been broken'. In his summing up prior to sentencing the Recorder disdained the systematic way in which 'the premises were regularly fitted up for the purpose'. He rejected the idea that the Howes should not be punished since they had 'ceased to carry on the nefarious trade' and commented on the reluctance of would-be prosecutors as follows:

> I can well understand that neighbours and parishioners are unwilling to take upon themselves the odium of prosecuting in cases of this kind, and I can also understand the motives of those who desired to prevent a public repetition of the details … this is the first prosecution of the kind that has been before the court and it is necessary that an example should be made of it.

Making the most of contemporary gender stereotypes, while claiming to draw no distinction between husband and wife he added the view that 'the woman who participates in an offence of this kind is worse than the man'.[19]

The Howe case is unusual for several reasons. It is clear that the initial hearing before the bench had intended not to air any details. The two solicitors defending and prosecuting agreed that they only needed the minimum of facts to transfer the case to Quarter Sessions. They said that they did not intend 'to weary the bench with the filthy details', that the house would be closed and the Howes moved on.[20] The Recorder, a local solicitor who would become town clerk in time, evidently decided to put such squeamishness to the test. His example was not followed in subsequent cases and the bench continued to obscure as many details of immoral conduct as they could. All these strategies do not conceal the fact that the magistrates were initially unable, given the state of the law then current and the power of those who did not wish to see their profits from alcohol consumption and prostitution reduced, to control the situation from the bench.

Controlling licensed premises
Each August and September the bench considered whether to confer or withhold spirit licences at their annual licensing day (and its several adjournments), known as the brewster session, and this represented potentially the height of their powers to control vice prior to 1885. During the period before the garrison arrived in 1856 the annual licensing meetings were routine, with only a handful of the 132 'places of public resort' attracting complaints and very few licences being suspended.[21] Abraham Garland, the landlord of the Sun public house in Maidenburgh Street, was taken to court in July 1853 for allowing fighting on the premises and for letting an apartment to 'a woman of ill fame'.[22] In this early period these kinds of story were reported in the *Essex Standard*, but the women were not named or overtly blamed for the presence

of prostitution. The magistrates responded to this nuisance in a variety of ways. First and foremost, they identified it as an indication of a contravention of the licence to serve alcohol. In publican Garland's case, the police constable reported the blood on the floor, the prostitute's apartment and the complaints of the neighbours. Garland's solicitor 'alluded to the want of experience of his client', an observation that was rejected by the magistrate, who remembered an earlier caution and who described the Sun as the worst public house in the town. But, having delivered this public condemnation, the mayor then *granted* the licence with a warning and a fine of £2 plus expenses. This mixed message emanating from the bench could be interpreted as a response to political pressures in the town around the selling and the drinking of alcohol, as explained below. But it could also be an expression of the town's leaders' generally laisse-faire attitude to vice or, at worst, an example of the hypocritical approach to prostitution deplored by Josephine Butler in her work in the 1870s to force the repeal of the CDAs.[23]

The problem increased as the garrison developed and the town responded to the soldiers' expectations that it would provide them with leisure opportunities outside the camp. In 1857 the solicitor Mr Goody, trying unsuccessfully to persuade the bench to grant a new licence for his brewer client Mr Daniell, set out some of the potential rules of engagement. Daniell, he said, 'on hearing that the town of Colchester was about to be made an important garrison town had, in common with other gentlemen, come forward most spiritedly and erected a large and commodious house near the Camp'. His was not the first public house to be built and he therefore accepted that he was not first in line for consideration. However, his house was larger and 'would be beneficial and conducive to the morals of the men and would in no way interfere with the trade of any other house'. Mr Daniell was suggesting that prostitutes would not be welcome in his public house, which would bear no resemblance to the squalid beerhouses elsewhere in the road. He had no other licence but was not a newcomer, 'having been connected with the town 38 years'. Mr Goody's parting shot was to point out the increase in the number of licences in the past year.[24] The magistrates were thus presented with a business model that attended to enterprise, reputation and fair competition, and these became their main criteria in succeeding annual licensing meetings when considering new applications. But when it came to reissuing licences, in the words of magistrate Dr Williams, 'the Bench had no wish to put themselves in opposition to the publicans', an approach which must also have affected how the police dealt with unruly houses.[25]

The result of this laissez-faire policy was that soon after the arrival of the garrison in 1856 the magistrates were faced in court with prostitutes charged with anti-social and criminal activities while the camp hospital filled with soldiers infected with venereal disease. In the 1860s the annual licensing days became busier as the police reported more complaints against beerhouses. The number of applications for new licences increased and the magistrates responded by refusing a proportion of them. Nevertheless, by 1865 there were 156 licensed premises, an increase of 17 per cent in just nine years. In February 1863 Colonel Guy wrote to the annual licensing meeting naming specific public houses that had been used by the 100 soldiers currently hospitalised with venereal disease. The bench expressed regret, yet, just six months later, it congratulated the trade on an excellent year and renewed every licence in town. The conservative *Standard* published a stinging rebuke, expressing astonishment at the complacency of the bench, accusing the magistrates of a miscarriage of justice and sympathising with the publicans of the well-run establishments. It claimed venereal disease had increased three-fold since February and that the disease 'recoils with ten-fold horror on the society which folds its hands in listlessness or guilty acquiescence – visiting the sins of the fathers upon the children to the third and fourth generation' – a biblical quote which would have been well-known to the paper's readers and a reference

Figure 20. Dr Edward Williams, honorary physician at the voluntary hospital and borough magistrate. He described himself, in the 1871 census, as 'JP, Alderman, MD Cambridge and lately physician'.

to the physical effects on babies born to syphilitic mothers. Magistrate Dr Edward Williams defended the bench, pointing out that it was the parish's responsibility to alert the authorities to the presence of 'houses of infamy and disorder', but he did it 'with personal sarcasm and animadversion', accusing the editor of 'sounding alarms of evil that can only be seen from his perverted and defective point of view'. The editor rebuked him for 'forgetting his position and its obligations' and advised him to cease to confer with the publicans 'who pleaded the necessity of the thing' and instead to attend to the garrison commander's specific complaints.[26]

Overall, their relaxed response to a serious problem suggests that the magistrates were acting as a collection of individuals more interested in maintaining their authority against the colonel's challenge than in acting decisively and effectively to reduce vice. For his part the colonel had distributed notices in the barrack huts threatening penalties to soldiers who allowed women to congregate there.[27] In 1868 the magistrates were made a laughing stock by a letter published in *The Times* gleefully reporting that the Colchester bench had sent a young girl to prison for 21 days 'for taking a sprig of lavender out of a garden'. The story was picked up by provincial newspapers and the clerk to the justices had to write to explain that she was 'a common woman of the town', a fact that had not been made explicit in the original court report.[28]

The magistrates' lack of decisive action did not win them respect. In 1867 at the annual brewster meeting the mayor read two 'memorials' from Anglican and nonconformist ministers deploring the 'lamentable increase in prostitution' and decided to consult the garrison again and to refuse a few old licences while granting two new ones. They admitted that they relied on the *owners* of public houses to control the problem, while the head constable said 'we can't hold the landlords responsible for what takes place outside their houses'.[29] The mayor, unwilling to blame the garrison, said the Borough had

> 117 public houses and 53 beer houses to a population in round numbers of 25,000, which would be one house to every 145 or 150 inhabitants, or one public house or beer house to every 30 houses … . Most of them or many of them are very little more than dens and traps to catch the soldiers. Women are kept in many of them to decoy the soldiers, who are drawn there by the attraction of women and by dancing and for the purposes of drinking the beverages sold by the landlord.

Despite this apparently negative attitude to some of the town's public houses, the numbers had now crept up to 170, a 9 per cent rise in two years. The mayor went on to talk defensively about 'hospital returns from the Camp and the Workhouse', which served to prove that their decision that day not to renew the licences of five public houses had been 'fully warranted' and supported by the military authorities and 'the clergy and ministers of other denominations'. In the same breath he reminded his audience that 'beerhouses are beyond the control of the Bench'.[30] This evidence suggests that the magistrates were concerned to uphold their own authority first and to ensure the police helped in this, but they justified their failure to exert real power by blaming weakness in the law and the craftiness of those who owned and ran the brothels. The lock hospital had not yet been built and the system of licensed prostitution under the CDAs not yet set up.

Controlling prostitutes and brothels

Under the law the bench could also fine and jail women for indecent acts performed in public – in a field or the street – and also for the vaguer crime of 'loitering', either in the street or in the beerhouse. Rebecca Alexander, who was supposedly 'of disreputable character', was arrested for 'loitering about on the pavement' in 1854 but escaped a harsh sentence, as the press coverage of her case noted:

> The Bench, although determined to suppress prostitution in the town, were unwilling to be too severe and on condition of her fulfilling her promise of leaving the town they would not convict her upon this charge, and another complaint of drunkenness and disorderly conduct should be allowed to stand over.[31]

So, in this case, as in the 1871 Pelham's Lane brothel case (see Chapter 8), the bench's proclaimed determination was trumped by the miscreant's promise to leave town. In fact only ten of the 337 women in our database were charged with soliciting, all in the period before the lock hospital opened. Four of them were dismissed or cautioned, the rest receiving a prison sentence with hard labour of at least a month.

The bench was empowered to punish women they found guilty of crimes associated with prostitution but, in the period before the lock hospital opened, they often decided not to. About a third of the prostitutes in this period managed to avoid being fined or imprisoned except perhaps for a night or two in the police cells. Sometimes the magistrates or the prosecutor accepted that this was punishment enough, another indication of a tendency to not deal harshly with immoral conduct. The police were expected to deal with disorderly behaviour. Mr Henry Wolton, magistrate and successful grocer, dealt with a breach of the peace case involving a 'disturbance among prostitutes in Black Boy Lane'. He noted that 'these women had recently become so disorderly, refusing to take the advice of the police when spoken to'. The prostitutes in this case were sentenced to an exemplary punishment of three weeks in the *county* house of correction in Chelmsford rather than the hospital closed its doors to prostitutes, Colchester's police brought the first brothel case to the magistrates – a portion of Bretts Buildings in Magdalen Street where three prostitutes lived. Shortly afterwards, in November 1886, Charles Wire, described by the head constable as 'an elderly respectable man', was in court to face the truth about his tenants in Childwell Alley, just behind the Lifeboat. Mr Prior, the solicitor defending Mr Wire, made a technical objection that 'disorderly houses were not identical with brothels, because although a brothel may be a disorderly house, every disorderly house was not a brothel'.[40] The magistrates were persuaded by this argument, and by Mr Wire's apparent respectability, and dismissed the case (see Chapter 4).[41] But Mr Prior's argument might be judged specious; the *Ipswich Journal*, reporting a case of brothel-keeping, quoted the Recorder's summing-up, in which he said 'he wished to make it clear to the Jury that although there might not be any fighting, robbery, or such disorder at the house, if it was kept for immoral purposes, that alone constituted disorder'.[42] The word 'disorder' thus covered flexible definitions of unacceptable behaviour, from noise and commotion caused by drunken customers to activities associated with crime and prostitution.

In July 1887 two premises in Burlington Road came before the court. The police had managed to clear No. 4 of Annette Wright, 'an unfortunate … who did knowingly permit those premises to be used as a brothel' but, since the girls had left town, the head constable recommended the case be dismissed. Three prostitutes were named, having admitted they had lodged with Annette and had taken people to the house. But their pimp, Jeremiah Collins, 29, a married labourer with two small children, who lived next door, was not dealt with so leniently, being fined £5 plus costs.[43]

In 1888 the focus shifted to Maidenburgh Street. In February the rector of the parish requested that two little girls be rescued from a house there 'of the vilest possible description … to all intents and purposes a brothel'. In October it was a row of 'four or five cottages … one room upstairs and one room down', owned by Samuel Brett, that was under the spotlight. We have already noted in Chapter 7 the head constable's reluctance to proceed against the girl, Emma Middleton, in this case. As for Brett, the newspaper does not make clear what the outcome was for him.

> The Chairman said the Bench considered this was a very serious matter indeed, and he must have been perfectly well aware that he was doing wrong, and would therefore be fined £10 and £1.7.6 costs … . Defendant said the property was mortgaged, and he could not pay. The Chairman said it was a crying evil that must be put a stop to.[44]

This case was also debated at length by the Board of Guardians when four of the girls who had been living in this brothel ended up in the Union workhouse.

Brett told the Guardians that 'the houses had been let to this sort of woman for 100 years ... he had had them 40 years himself and they had been let to these people ... the places would not command respectable tenants'. The Guardians were not unanimous in condemning this state of affairs; the chairman observed that the Board was being 'kind' to Mr Brett and one of the board agreed, saying, 'Mr Brett must let his houses and these women must live somewhere'. However, another strongly objected:

> It was extraordinary that a Guardian should offer arguments for letting these cottages in this way. He supposed the income from these cottages would be about 1s 6d per week and the town was saddled with the expenses in connection with these girls who came into the Union amounting to £20.[45]

The final word was solicitor Mr Church's, who said that the Board had no control over this matter at all.

In February 1889 Childwell Alley was back under the spotlight. Not only had a deserting soldier been picked up in a brothel there, but three prostitutes were in court and fined for being tenants of another brothel in the Alley. The prostitute who 'was the most to blame, she being responsible for the rent' (even though her 'assumed husband' had hired the house) was fined twice the amount of the other women involved.[46] In March 1890 'the worst case that had ever been before the bench' was heard. It featured John Sargeant, a chimney sweep, his brothel in Newton's Yard, and some police evidence judged by the *Standard* to be too shocking to reveal. Sargeant was sentenced to two months with hard labour.[47] In November of the same year George Game, coffee-house keeper, was heavily fined (£10 plus costs) for hosting a brothel in Queen Street.[48] In October 1891 the Anchor Inn, Magdalen Street, owned by the Colchester Brewing Company and tenanted by William Collins, came under surveillance for misdoings in the back yard. Despite Henry Jones's best efforts, Collins was fined £5 with costs.[49]

In March 1892 more 'Shocking Revelations at Colchester' were revealed by the *Standard*. Sarah Ann McNeal, a married woman with two children whose husband was away, occupied premises next to the Beehive on North Hill. She was charged with allowing her premises to be used as a brothel. According to the police reports, a regular stream of soldiers and civilians made their way there for half-hourly appointments. Sarah was sentenced to two months with hard labour. She was led from court sobbing hysterically: 'Oh don't put me away sir. What will my children do?' The Beehive's landlady was also in trouble for supplying beer to Sarah's brothel. She was fined £5 with costs.[50] A week later another woman was charged with brothel keeping at No. 42 Magdalen Street. The head constable discussed the responsibility of the tenant, the agent and the owner under the law. The agent said the woman had presented herself as being on the brink of marriage to a corporal in the Army Service Corps. The constable agreed they had been engaged, but said 'they were too poor to marry'.[51] The newspaper did not report the outcome. Perhaps she was forgiven.

In May 1893 the focus shifted back to North Hill and the Marquis of Granby's yard, where Kate Lambert's brothel was discovered. She had moved there, with Polly Alexander and Lizzie Brown, from previous brothels in Northgate Street and Maidenburgh Street. For some undisclosed reason, and despite Kate's brothel-keeping career, the bench was 'inclined to deal leniently with [the] defendant, in the hope that afterwards she would follow some more respectable living'. They imposed a fine of £2 with costs.[52] In March 1894 Harry Stone was convicted of keeping a disorderly house at No. 192 Magdalen Street. Not only was it disorderly in housing three prostitutes, but it was described as being in an 'abominable filthy state'.[53]

So, thanks to a significant change in the law, in the space of 14 years Colchester's police and magistrates felt confident enough to confront 14 cases involving individuals implicated in the provision of brothels, many more than they had in the whole of the previous 40 years. Only five prostitutes were arrested in connection with these sweeps. Colchester's prostitutes certainly came under close scrutiny, the sordid routines of their working lives timed and counted by constables hanging around in yards, peeping at windows, talking to neighbours and keeping track of who came into town and who left. But few of them were arrested as common prostitutes in this connection, as the police were in pursuit of the landlords and pimps. And, while engaged in snooping, they were arresting more drunk and disorderly prostitutes than in the earlier periods.

However, the brothel cases also show that, new legislation notwithstanding, an element of leniency remained the order of the day. In many cases the bench pointed out that they could, had they wished, have dealt more severely with the publicans and the women. Both police and magistrates understood the potential in the system for misunderstandings as well as for calculated profiteering from vice. The presence of children in brothels seems to have worried the authorities. For instance, the chimney sweep's story above – apparently too shocking to be revealed in full – was followed up a week later with the story of his 'bright little boy of seven years ... utterly neglected by his father and mother', whom the head constable brought into court to recommend 'arrangements being made for his reception into an Industrial School'. Perhaps the little boy was downcast, for the Mayor took the occasion to urge the child to 'be good and learn all he could at the School, and get on and be a man'.[54]

Conclusion

So, did Colchester's magistrates exhibit the traits claimed by Sir James Munby in this chapter's opening quotation? Did they promote virtue and discourage vice? Was their view of sexual morality narrow? The arrival of the garrison certainly tested the bench to the limit, but their response to the pressure from the garrison and the town's moral reformers evolved slowly. Many historians have concluded that, in the eighteenth century, when the bench operated without the support of a police force, their peacekeeping duties were paramount.[55] They had to have sufficient local knowledge to be able to avert riot before it began and they managed this feat of authority (rather than power) by carefully balancing the needs of justice against the powerful effects of mercy. Tracing how their powers changed following changes in the law and the provision of a national police force demonstrates very clearly the pressures, including the scrutiny of the press and party political interests, affecting the bench in this developing Victorian garrison town where their authority was increasingly criticised in the press. Their main line of defence was that they could only work within the law and some laws were weak. But, as the *Standard* observed,

> whilst the law remains in its present state the magistrates alone can effectually grapple with the evils of the system, and we believe that if they were earnestly desirous of doing so, the police could, without much difficulty, supply them with sufficient evidence upon which to act.[56]

They had wide discretionary powers and, according to Sindall, magistrates 'could be ruthless in their efforts to stamp out certain forms of behaviour'.[57] However, it is difficult to find examples of ruthlessness emanating from the Colchester borough courts and the *Standard* editor's accusation that the bench colluded with publicans seems a reasonable conclusion.

Until the lock hospital opened in 1869 the bench's approach was to make stern pronouncements while dismissing a third of prostitute court cases and granting most applications for alcohol licences. Their approach could be described as flexible, as the stated determination to suppress prostitution translated into punishments for only two-thirds of the women. The men who bought the services of a prostitute did not always get away scot-free either, some being named and rebuked and, occasionally, arrested and punished for violent behaviour. But, over the following 17 years, when the lock hospital was in situ, the bench was dealing on average with at least one crime involving a prostitute every month and they were encountering repeat offenders. Their punishments for prostitutes were more severe and new alcohol licences were *apparently* under greater scrutiny, although their numbers still increased. Only after the closure of the lock hospital (which coincided with a change in the law in 1885) was any sustained effort made to clear the town's brothels. This *pattern* of change, firmly based on the introduction of new laws, can be recovered from the evidence, although we have found no sign the bench drew attention to it in public. While one or two of the magistrates were very keen to reduce the number of licences and made comments about what they saw as they walked the streets, all the others expected businesses to police themselves and were impatient with suggestions that seemed to erode their authority.

Usually the magistrates were not reported scolding the women for their immoral behaviour. They were more concerned by whether they had offended before, whether they had assaulted the arresting constable, whether they made promises to reform or to leave town, and whether their brief could find enough holes in the evidence to cast doubt on their guilt. This gives the impression that the magistrates' views were not narrow but that they were either tolerant of promiscuity or anxious to draw a veil over it (or perhaps both). The presence and contribution of medical magistrates on the bench may have affected their approach to morality. As we saw in Chapter 2, the doctors who served the poor were anxious not to condemn neglectful mothers. The medics who appeared before the borough coroner's inquests were also generally not judgemental when asked to give opinions on human behaviour. As we have seen, the bench sometimes called upon its medical magistrates to deliver specific information about the CDAs and their scientific knowledge and professional assurance may have influenced decision-making in court. Occasionally the bench was caught on the back foot, as in 1882, when a 33-year-old prostitute named Mary Ann Golding (previously mentioned in Chapters 4, 5 and 7) came before them charged with being found drunk in St John's Street the previous night. The mayor (chairman of the bench) recognised her because

> from the age of 16 she had been constantly going in and out of prison. She had had month upon month. She had had six months and twelve months, and other sentences, and now she was before the court for the sixteenth time. The Bench scarcely knew what to do with her, but they had made up their minds not to send her to jail, but to send her home, and if anything could be done to extricate her from the state in which she now was the Bench would be only too happy.[58]

Mary Ann, or Blossom as she was known, left the court a free woman, the bench washing its hands of her. She had begun her career from the workhouse in 1866, where she was considered to be an imbecile by the medical officer (who subsequently became a magistrate), and she is last seen in the primary sources in 1885 in a brothel run by Ishmael Clark, witnessing another prostitute stabbing him. Between these two dates the magistrates had sentenced her to between two and three years in jail in total and she had also spent time in the Union workhouse and, in all probability, the lock hospital. She was incorrigible, responsible for several thefts and for many drunken and riotous scenes where windows were broken, obscenities shouted and threats issued. She threw missiles at constables, refused to be led home quietly, instead throwing herself down in the road saying she did not care what became of her, indulged in hysterics when in court and eventually allowed herself to be controlled by a notorious pimp. Under the law authority could do nothing about a girl trading her sexual favours from her own lodgings and the magistrates eventually accepted that their best efforts had failed.

Only in the 1890s did the magistrates grasp the nettle of trying to reduce the number of brothels. The women responded to this initiative by operating out of private lodgings and being prepared to move on when constables began hovering about outside taking notes. But the incidence of female vagrancy in Colchester increased substantially in these final years of the nineteenth century and a large number of these vagrants were prostitutes.

Notes

1. Catherine Woodham, accused of stealing a pair of boots from the Co-op in Long Wyre Street, said she had stolen them for a poor widow and that she 'did it with a good heart'. *ES* 18 January 1890.
2. *The Times* 30 October 2013.
3. Martin, *The Story of Colchester*, p. 90.
4. Durgan, *Colchester, 1835–1992*, p. 182.
5. *ES* 5 March 1862.
6. The Summary Jurisdiction Act (1848) required magistrates to sit in pairs. The mayor said that the number of magistrates was 'inadequate to the demands upon them; for some of them living on the outskirts of the borough, and others having professional engagements to attend to, the public business had been many times delayed from inability to secure the attendance of a second magistrate'. *ES* 13 November 1857.
7. *ES* 11 December 1886.
8. *ES* 28 April 1858.
9. *ES* 13 June 1891.
10. *IJ* 5 September 1885.
11. *ES* 19 August 1857.
12. *ES* 28 February 1855.
13. *ES* 21 July 1858.
14. A few are reported receiving a reprimand from the bench, but the words spoken are not recorded.
15. *ES* 17 June 1857.
16. *ES* 22 September 1854.
17. *ES* 21 September 1866.
18. The report added that 'the house of one Rumsey, living in Sir Isaac's Walk, also required strict

watch, especially on market days; and the Superintendent would inform the Bench from time to time of the parties who attended these places'. *ES* 4 August 1854.
19   *ES* 7 April 1871.
20   *ES* 17 February 1871.
21   These were 94 public houses with spirit licences, 38 beer houses and the camp canteen. *ES* 29 September 1858. Five years previously it was reported there were 88 public houses.
22   *ES* 8 July 1853.
23   Bartley, *Prostitution*; Petrie, *A Singular Iniquity*.
24   *ES* 9 September 1857.
25   *ES* 5 September 1856.
26   *ES* 18 September and 2 October 1863.
27   *ES* 1 November 1865 reported a forthcoming court martial on a farrier sergeant 'for having a private soldier and some prostitutes in his room' contrary to the notices put up on Colonel White's orders.
28   *The Times* 15 September 1868; the story of prostitute Victoria Harmer's crime is revealed in *ES* 31 August 1868 and further discussed in *ES* 16 and 23 September 1868.
29   *ES* 28 August 1868.
30   *ES* 20 September 1867. At this date beerhouse owners applied for a licence from the excise authority.
31   *ES* 11 August 1854.
32   *ES* 7 February 1866.
33   Brown, *Colchester*, p. 168.
34   The following month Emma Hall and Eliza Radford were also said to be 'the first charge of this kind since the adoption of the CDAs'. They both served a sentence with hard labour. *ES* 30 April 1869.
35   *ES* 1 October 1881.
36   *ES* 10 March 1869.
37   *ES* 19 September 1869. This retrograde attitude was upheld in 1885 when the British Hotel's 20 years of immoral business was challenged at the annual licensing meeting. *ES* 3 October 1885.
38   The borough jail had a medical officer who was one of the town's general practitioners. Perhaps he prescribed remedies for syphilitic prostitute inmates.
39   John Conniff, aged 38, committed suicide in the camp hospital while being treated for venereal disease. *ES* 28 October 1859. See Chapter 6 for a description of the symptoms of syphilis.
40   *ES* 13 November 1886.
41   When Mr Wire died Mr Prior acquired the properties and also had problems with immoral tenants.
42   *IJ* 9 January 1892.
43   *ES* 16 July 1887.
44   *ES* 27 October 1888.
45   *ES* 18 and 25 August 1888.
46   *ES* 7 February 1889.
47   *ES* 15 March 1890.
48   *ES* 29 November 1890.
49   *ES* 17 October 1891.
50   *ES* 5 March 1892.
51   *ES* 12 March 1892.
52   *ES* 6 May 1893.
53   *ES* 10 March 1894.
54   *ES* 22 March 1890.

55 D. Hay *et al.*, *Albion's Fatal Tree: Crime and Society in Eighteenth-century England* (London, 1975); E.P. Thompson, *Whigs and Hunters: The Origin of the Black Act* (London, 1975).
56 *ES* 28 September 1866.
57 Sindall, *Street Violence*, p. 151. In 1859 a drunken woman was 'forgiven' by the bench as she appeared on the new clerk's inaugural day. *ES* 22 July 1859.
58 *ES* 23 September 1882.

CHAPTER 10

The Ship at Headgate

*All he wanted was that they should
close at 11 o'clock at night.*[1]

The last four chapters have considered prostitution from the perspective of the army's attempt to control venereal disease through the CDAs and the developing role of the town's police, solicitors and magistrates. This chapter attempts to link these endeavours to the experience of the town's reformers (described in the next chapter) through a case study of an old-established public house in Colchester. In this case study we discuss in some detail a series of licensing decisions taken in connection with just one public house in Colchester that was shaken out of its calm routine by the arrival of the garrison. The problems posed by a disorderly house at the more respectable end of town were not the same as those experienced by the Lifeboat and the Anchor in the disreputable back streets. The Ship was not associated with thieving or fighting, but it did produce excessive noise that annoyed its prosperous neighbours.

The Ship at Headgate had its frontage on St John's Street and its back entrance on Butt Road. It had been an inn since the seventeenth century and had a large yard at the back with stabling for up to 60 horses.[2] It was a favourite establishment for farmers coming into town from the Maldon direction and had been run by John Seaborne and his wife Catharine since at least the 1820s, until the recently widowed John gave up the licence in 1859 at the age of 80.[3] The Ship would never be the same again. Its clientele changed from farmers to soldiers; from hosting Conservative Club dinners it began providing farewell suppers for battalions departing to foreign fields.[4] In the next ten years its licence changed hands no fewer than eight times, a sure sign of a disorderly house. It became known for music and dancing in an upstairs room and its neighbours began to suffer disturbances and noise, both from within the Ship and in the street outside. When the renewal of the licence was contested in

1865 the landlord blamed the presence of two particular regiments for extra noise, adding that 'he had had no disturbance inside the house; he could not help what was done outside'. Even though one of the magistrates said he had seen soldiers fighting in the house, the bench renewed the licence without further ado.[5]

The problems came to a head in 1867. In August of that year, just one week before the annual licensing day, the licence of the Ship was transferred from Charles Rayner to John Eaden in a final panicky attempt to forestall troublesome accusations of disorderly conduct in the house. The licensing meeting started late because the bench had more paperwork to discuss than usual. The rural dean and a group of clergy from several independent churches had written two letters begging the bench to check the progress of immorality in the town and asking them not to give new licences in areas of the town already well endowed with public houses. The mayor, under this pressure, had collected additional information from the garrison and, as a result, the bench selected 13 'houses more or less frequented by soldiers' for special consideration. The Ship was on the list. Perhaps on the strength of the newly installed tenant the bench decided to renew the Ship's licence, but on the strict understanding that the music and dancing, which caused annoyance to neighbours, was abated. When the new landlord began to protest the mayor cut him off, saying 'You had better not argue the question'.

The following year, 1868, there was yet another new landlord at the Ship, Ben Ram, who evidently had not heeded the caution. For a second time the bench was unable to come to a decision about whether to grant the licence and the discussion had to be adjourned. This time the solicitor, Mr Philbrick, admitted that the owners (Messrs Osborne, brewers) feared that Ram was endangering the licence – he 'had conducted himself in a way that was not creditable', which included sheltering an army deserter – and asked the bench to consider granting the licence to an agent while a better tenant was sought. The bench was not persuaded by Mr Philbrick's eloquence, and no doubt feared that his request was the thin end of a substantial wedge that other solicitors would use in their future requests for licences. The Ship's spirit licence was withdrawn and the inn reduced to a beerhouse.

For 12 months the Ship's takings were substantially reduced while yet another landlord, under strict instructions to redeem its reputation, did his best to quell disturbances. His neighbours enjoyed quieter times. Messrs Osborne's agent had selected William Pettitt as landlord, who had successfully run the Lion at Kirby-le-Soken for many years and who, the following year, reapplied for the spirit licence. Solicitor Mr Philbrick rolled out the usual list of arguments in favour – that it was unfair to punish the owner for a bad tenant, that the venerable Ship was much missed by visitors (who wanted to drink spirits) and that the owners had good-heartedly kept it on as a beerhouse with an unexceptionable tenant who had the support of many of his neighbours. But he had to face the opposing solicitor Mr Goody, himself a resident of Head Street, representing a rival brewer, Messrs Cobbold, who claimed:

> the house was badly conducted and ladies and others could not pass by on their way to a place of worship or elsewhere without having their ears polluted by language unfit to be heard coming from soldiers and girls who were sitting upstairs with the windows wide open. When passing he had seen girls dancing and sitting with their arms round soldiers' necks and with a spirit licence this could be continued till midnight instead of 11 o'clock.[6]

Mr Philbrick's rejoinder was that soldiers were allowed to drink in licensed premises and that not every woman therein was of bad repute. He was supported by magistrate Dr Williams, who observed that 'it was very rare that a magistrate felt called upon to notice the remarks of an advocate in a court' and he was surprised that Mr Goody had not alerted the police to the disgraceful behaviour he claimed to have witnessed. Mr Goody had no answer to that and he and Dr Williams exchanged ill-tempered jibes like boys in a schoolyard. However, when the Ship's *beer* licence was discussed minutes later the bench had some encouraging remarks for the landlord, Mr Pettitt:

> The Mayor in granting the application advised the applicant to determine to carry on the house in a way to give no cause of complaint. Mr Hawkins – Let it be conducted in such a way that we may have much pleasure in granting you a full licence next year.

In the event the bench was split, four magistrates being willing to renew the spirit licence and four not, and the decision was therefore adjourned in the hope that some time for reflection and a renewed discussion might affect the voting.

When the adjourned meeting was held several weeks later Mr Philbrick, who was abroad, was represented by Mr Jones, who came to court armed with a memorial 'most numerously and respectably signed, recommending Mr Pettitt as a fit and proper person to be entrusted with a spirit licence'. Mr Goody, opposing the application, argued that the bench 'had already in effect refused it on the ground that they refused that of smaller houses in the bye streets of the town if they were the resort of soldiers and loose women'. He followed up this refutable claim by suggesting that the names on Mr Jones' memorial were in many cases not parishioners and that the granting of a spirit licence would increase the late-night misery of the neighbours to an even later hour than currently. Mr Goody then called several of the neighbours to give evidence.

Figure 21. Headgate, where surgeon Mr Norman and solicitor Mr Goody were disturbed by the customers' antics at the Ship.

One of the neighbours was surgeon John Norman, who had occupied a house on the corner of Head Street opposite the Ship since the late 1830s. His wife was a teacher and she was recorded in the 1841 and 1861 censuses as running a boarding school for teenage girls in the house. Mr Norman said that during his first 20 years in Head Street he had not once been disturbed, but that during the ensuing 15 years – in other words, since the arrival of the garrison in Colchester – 'rows had been regularly occurring'. He complained that

> a great many soldiers and loose women frequented the house and caused much disturbance after 11 o'clock at night. He had seen women take the placard boards from the front of The Ship and dance on them in the middle of the street swearing and creating a great disturbance.

He had had to get himself out of bed and resort to the police station in the High Street to ask for a constable to intervene. His chief anxiety was that a renewal of the spirit licence would mean that the Ship would not need to observe the 11pm closing time observed by beerhouses.

Mr Jones pressed Mr Norman for any evidence that he might have of business being carried on at the Ship after 11pm. 'Name an instance where persons returned to the house after the doors were closed?' This was beyond

Mr Norman's powers of recall. He answered doubtfully, 'I can't swear they were the same persons; I heard the doors close and saw the people outside. The disturbance took place in the public road, opposite my window.' He agreed with Mr Jones that they might have been lodgers returning to the house and also that William Pettitt had been a satisfactory landlord. Mr Jones then cleverly increased the uncertainty in Mr Norman's evidence.

> Mr Jones – And have you not signed in favour of another person a short distance off in the same street having a spirit licence?
> Witness (Mr Norman) – Yes (Laughter).
> Mr Jones – So you have not so much thoughtfulness and consideration for your neighbours as you have for yourself?
> Witness – Anyone would do the same.[7]

Mr Jones also demolished the next witness, Mr Beard, who had an ironmonger's shop next door to the Ship. He claimed to have seen 'acts of indecency unfit to be mentioned', but, under pressure, was unwilling and then unable to provide any details. The mayor tried to help him out by suggesting he might perhaps have seen 'familiarities'? Mr Beard accepted this assistance and said he had seen 'soldiers pulling women about outside the house'. Mr Jones pounced on his inability to recall indecent acts *inside* the house. Turning to the bench, he 'submitted that there was nothing inside the "case" presented by his friend Mr Goody. One witness had contradicted the other most materially and together they went to prove his side of the question.' The police had lodged no complaints over the year, disputes in the street were in a public space, there had been no bench opposition to granting a beerhouse licence to the Ship and Mr Jones' confident recommendation was therefore that the magistrates should respond to their own sense of 'right and justice'.

The bench tried to pick some holes in Mr Jones' case. The mayor asked if the parish vicar and churchwardens had signed the memorial (they hadn't). Mr Tabor asked the head constable if he was aware of any complaints against the Ship (he wasn't, and was unable to confirm Mr Norman's account of his late-night visit to the police station). Mr Jones discussed the individuals who had signed the memorial and 'further dwelt on the sufficient punishment inflicted on the owners and occupier by the house being deprived of a spirit licence for two years', but in vain. The bench withdrew to discuss and returned with a majority decision to reject the licence application. Mr Jones immediately lodged an appeal.

Three weeks later the case came up again at the county Quarter Sessions in Chelmsford. Two county magistrates were on the bench and barristers presented the opposing arguments. This time the witnesses had had time to embellish their accounts. Mr Norman now described indecencies he had seen from his upstairs window and Mr Beard claimed not to be able to use some of the rooms in his house because the noise from the Ship was so loud. Various innuendos to do with Messrs Osborne's business dealings with witnesses and magistrates were made by both barristers with a view to invalidating the evidence. The head constable was induced to flounder over his contribution, agreeing that he sometimes forgot salient facts and that the women who consorted with soldiers were not necessarily prostitutes, as 'some of the soldiers who frequented the house were most respectable'. Satisfied neighbours were also put on the stand and, as a result, the Quarter Sessions reversed the borough court decision. The Ship regained its spirit licence.[8]

Over the course of 40 years the Ship had, like the town itself, presented a respectable face to the world. It fed and watered local farmers and their horses and any customers wanting to spend time with a prostitute would have had to repair to one of the town's discreet brothels off the High Street. The arrival of the garrison in 1856 was a huge challenge to discretion and respectability and the Ship's progress reflected these changing circumstances. It lay on the route into town taken by the cavalry, whose barracks were built further up Butt Road in the early 1860s. Its upper room was a convenient meeting place for soldiers with time to kill and before long the Ship's landlords were providing entertainments to encourage the soldiers to linger for longer, employing musicians and allowing 'loose' women to congregate. The provision of gaiety at the Ship was replicated in many other public houses in the town.

The gaiety was brought to a sudden halt in 1867 with the threat of the loss of the spirit licence. This would not have occurred without pressure upon the bench from a number of sources: first, the garrison, anxious about the unacceptable rates of venereal disease; second, the Anglican and nonconformist churches, seeking to reduce immorality and prostitution; third, competing brewers; and, fourth, the Ship's neighbours, who wanted to sleep at night. Pressure to control the Ship did not *originate* with the police or the magistrates. The Ship was not a brothel and was never accused of harbouring prostitutes by providing rooms for them to take customers to, so was not vulnerable from that direction. It was not a new business, although its clientele had changed, so could not be refused a licence on the grounds of being an addition to a superfluity of licensed premises in the area. Thus, initially (in 1867) the licence was renewed with a caution to the landlord to reduce the emanating racket. This was also a warning to the Ship's owner, who responded by changing the tenant yet again. This was the borough magistrates' default position: to assume that a tolerant response would be met halfway by more acceptable behaviour. Perhaps this eighteenth-century approach had once worked well in Colchester, but it was no longer appropriate in a garrison town.

In 1868 the Ship's licence was revoked not as a response to moral objections but on a technicality – because there was no tenant in situ. But when it was time to reapply for the spirit licence about 11 months later, the bench had their decision making steered by opposing solicitors representing brewers whose business was much valued by the town. The solicitors (as explained in a previous chapter) presented strongly opposing arguments, Mr Philbrick giving the bench four good reasons to follow their natural tolerant instincts to support business and encourage acceptable behaviour, while Mr Goody (who lived in Head Street) appealed to any magistrate with a moral conscience who had ever been kept up at night by inconsiderate neighbours. Between them the solicitors succeeded in bringing about a stalemate, with the bench equally and awkwardly divided. This, no doubt, was the reason for one magistrate's odd claim, spoken in open court, that they took no notice of what the solicitors said. In such a case the rules called for an adjournment and a chance for the solicitors to rethink their presentation and for the magistrates to reconsider and sometimes to seek evidence for themselves or to put pressure on recalcitrant colleagues. As described above, when the two solicitors brought fresh evidence to the adjourned meeting the witnesses against renewing the licence floundered when asked for exact details of nuisances and were made to look foolish in court (as were the police). It may well have been this *lèse majesté* that ensured the bench voted to suspend the licence for a second year and which also ensured the likelihood of success on appeal.

The account of the Ship's fate well illustrates the changing attitudes in the developing town and the public contest between professional men – magistrates, medical men and solicitors – that up to this point had never been exposed quite so brutally in the context of licensing decisions. As we saw in the last chapter, it was this inability or reluctance to challenge the general acceptance of the status quo that made any control of prostitution difficult to agree and which had an impact on how the police responded. The moralists had to deal with accusations that reducing licensed premises took away many livelihoods (and increased the poor rate), while the pragmatists were often those acquiring money or status from successful trading, however disreputable it might be. Solicitors found the bench easy to discompose by appealing, sometimes ironically, to the magistrates' natural sense of justice. The bench was keen to bluff its way out of public recrimination if possible, pontificating and blustering and making moral pronouncements. When annoyed, the magistrates retaliated, as shown above, by contradicting the solicitor, by interrogating their evidence and witnesses or, in the last analysis, by pulling rank. Only when the law changed in 1885 was any concerted effort made to reduce the number of brothels.

Notes

1. Surgeon John Norman's plea at the annual licensing day; *ES* 1 October 1869.
2. Jephcott says it was licensed in the seventeenth century. Jephcott, *The Inns, Taverns and Pubs of Colchester*, pp. 81–3.
3. *Pigot's Directory of Essex* (London, 1822); *ES* 2 November 1859.
4. *ES* 15 September 1832 and 30 July 1862.
5. *ES* 15 September 1865.
6. *ES* 27 August 1869.
7. *ES* 1 October 1869.
8. Within two or three years a large dancing room was built behind the Ship. Its name was changed to the Elephant and Castle and it became a music hall. Over the next 20 years nearly a dozen of the prostitutes on our database were arrested for fighting there.

CHAPTER 11

Reformers and neighbours

*(Voices – 'Go home Jessie!
Take your dirty tracts home!')*[1]

For Colchester's respectable families the evidence of the town's vice trade was everywhere to be seen, should they be inclined to look. Brothels existed inside the town walls in many places, including Maidenburgh Street, Pelham's Lane, Trinity Street, North Hill and Queen Street, and outside the walls in Vineyard Street, Magdalen Street, Osborne Street and Priory Street. The women lived and worked all over town, inside and outside the old Roman walls. Their places of resort existed in almost every parish.

Colchester's professional families – medical, legal, clergy – and businessmen also lived and worked all over the town, although most chose to live in the western half. It was impossible for them to avoid prostitutes going about their business in broad daylight or meandering home from the beerhouse late at night, and some of them encountered prostitutes in need of medical or legal assistance. As we saw in Chapter 10, solicitor Henry Goody and surgeon John Norman both lived in Head Street and endured the increasing racket emanating from the Ship. Both made half-hearted attempts to limit the disruption and others of the town's elite, the clergy included, seem to have done the same on occasion. Others must have been aware – even if they did no more than read the *Essex Standard* every week – of some very irregular behaviour taking place in any street in town and also of the very poor living standards endured by many of their neighbours.

As with any intractable social problem, the causes and solutions were seen to be many and various by the various authorities. Perhaps the reluctance of employers to pay a living wage, particularly to their youngest female workers, lay at the heart of their apparently tolerant attitude to vice. Many of them employed girls from poor families and expected them to behave decently and deferentially in a culture where most women were second-class citizens. Their wives were well aware of these girls' lack of moral and practical education. Poverty was accepted by many of the elite as a fact of life rather than a political problem in need of a solution. The poor laws dealt with paupers; the merely poor shifted for themselves, relying on neighbourliness and charity from time to time. Paula Bartley has written that 'women became prostitutes because they had no close relative to provide them with moral and financial support'.[2] But some in Victorian Colchester reversed this view with the idea, frequently expressed, that the girl who became a prostitute was vulnerable because she was poor, ignorant and targeted by unscrupulous men.

How did Colchester's more respectable inhabitants deal with what they saw as the public parade of immorality? Colchester had 16 parishes whose Anglican clergy were mostly resident in the town. There were also a similar number of nonconformist chapels with resident ministers.[3] The evidence suggests that very few clergy were willing to do practical work in public to reduce the vice trade, most preferring to shelter behind, or to encourage, a committee of women who did the difficult work of trying to befriend the parish's 'unfortunates' or, more often, divert a girl from a route into prostitution. When there were public lectures requesting support for some prostitute-reforming initiative the clergy were well represented in the audience and some revealed they were knowledgeable about the trade. For instance, a meeting in Norwich called to propose the setting-up of a female penitentiary for Norfolk and Suffolk had an audience in which clergy predominated. One of them, the Reverend S.J. Rigaud, observed:

> In Ipswich, the person who collected the statistics had only set down those persons as prostitutes who derived their entire support from the wages of sin, and had taken no account of the very large class who partially derived their means of subsistence from the same sources.[4]

Perhaps this female double life helped to conceal the extent of the problem for some observers and also to allow some to be uncertain about the definition of 'prostitute'.

The clergy had a public voice in their sermons and parish work and also commonly chaired the regular parish vestry meeting. We have found only one local sermon that may have addressed the town's prostitution problems, but occasionally a clergyman was reported speaking in a fatherly way to a tea party of little girls.[5] We can also hear the clergy speaking through the letters they sometimes wrote to the *Standard* and the bench, and have already quoted a selection of these in previous chapters. In 1841, well before the arrival of the garrison, Reverend Meshach Seaman began to campaign against immorality.

being that she had become the man's mistress. In his letter Seaman wrote at length about his experience as Union chaplain, meeting young prostitutes who expressed 'deepest regret for the first false steps taken by them' and sorrow for the 'disgrace and wretchedness incurred thereby'. He had no doubt that such misery was caused by 'want of the exercise of proper parental authority' in terms of both moral education and careful choice of employer. He ended this letter by quoting at length from a government report entitled 'The Training of Pauper Girls for Domestic Service', which claimed that girls leaving pauper schools were stunted physically and morally and that the system was 'an utter failure' because it ended 'almost invariably in physical and moral deterioration, and in the quick ruin of more than one half at or soon after their first start in life'.[17] Seaman's letter was entirely concerned with cautioning parents and young females, who were expected to be responsible for their own choices and demeanour. He even blamed an 'overweening desire to live in London' on the girl's vain ambition – 'imagining that greater respectability attaches to London than to country servitude' – rather than a simple hope of improving her wages and servitude. The letter makes no mention of the man's responsibility for taking advantage of the female vulnerability he described. In addition, Reverend Seaman expressed only 'astonishment' (rather than disgust) at a social system that produced stunted pauper children vulnerable to seduction and abandonment.

Towards the end of the century another crusading parson's voice was heard in Colchester. Reverend George Brown of St Botolph parish was active in trying to get the Childwell Alley brothels closed in 1895. He interviewed the prostitutes and brought their story before the Board of Guardians the following week:

> Susannah Schell said she had lived under Mrs Cornish in Barn Yard in a single room, at a rent of 4s 1d, which was paid nightly – 7d a night. Rebecca Munson said she lived under Mrs Cornish at 3, Barn Yard and removed to Childwell Alley because the people quarrelled over her head in Barn Yard. Annie Harris lived with Mrs Cornish in Barn Yard at a rent of 4s 1d per week. Annie Smith lived at 7 Childwell Alley up to Xmas last; she lived in Childwell Alley, that was to say, about a year and nine months. About last Xmas she removed to Barn Yard.

Annie's room was, he said, furnished with three chairs, a table, cups, saucers, plates and a teapot. Perhaps he thought it improper to mention the bed. Brown felt strongly that they should find out the name of the owner of the property and publish it.

> It seemed to him that the law was failing to reach this social evil in Colchester and the only hope was that public opinion might be brought to bear upon those who were making

money in that disgraceful way and that thus public opinion might do what the law had failed to do.[18]

The following week a letter was published in the newspaper from solicitor Asher Prior, the owner of the properties in question, as described in Chapter 4, explaining that he had set Mrs Cornish up as his rent collector and that she dealt with troublesome tenants. For her part, Mrs Cornish denied all the facts presented to the Board by Reverend Brown.[19] In the 50 years of our study these two clergymen are the only ones to make such detailed views public in this way. The others, while attending meetings and paying subscriptions to the relevant causes, were reluctant to air their views quite so publicly.

The Colchester Town Mission was another initiative which, like the Penitent Female Refuge, pre-dated the arrival of the garrison. It was set up in 1839 by two of Colchester's Independent chapels. It employed a town missionary who was employed to run it, no doubt with the practical support of his wife, from premises in Magdalen Street that included a chapel and a library. In 1858 it was reported that Mr Bartlett, town missionary, 'had made 5,646 domiciliary visits and had distributed 5,322 tracts during the year besides holding 175 meetings for exhortation and prayer'.[20] In 1861 his duties included 'rescuing unhappy females from their degradation and ruin'.[21] In 1859 the Mission expanded by forming the Colchester Female Mission, with one bible woman employed under a committee of 12 ladies, half from the established church and half from other denominations. This 'earnest female worker', Mrs Smith, served for 23 years on the north side of town.[22] By 1876 funds were raised to employ a second bible woman to 'be employed specially to devote her attention to Magdalen Street and that quarter of the Town'. Their duties were not specified in the Mission annals beyond 'visiting from house to house'. In 1877, when Elizabeth Coe was before the bench for being disorderly in the Rose and Crown, she was saved by

> a lady, who is a Bible woman of the Female Mission, (who) said she had the defendant under her notice for upwards of 12 months, and believed she was on the point of renouncing the immoral life she had for some considerable time been leading. Upon this lady promising to exercise surveillance over her, the Bench discharged her with a caution.[23]

The following year, when Elizabeth was charged with a similar offence, it was stated that efforts made to reclaim her had proved ineffectual.[24] In the 1880s a Mrs Brand set up a Band of Hope to engage local children, which developed into another Town Mission enterprise with the help of other ladies not afraid to work in 'such an unsavoury locality'.[25] The Mission women also collected statistics on poverty, reporting in 1895 that there were 800 men out of work in the town and of the pressing need to set up a soup kitchen.[26]

Figure 22. Mrs Louisa Round's Refuge for Fallen Women, Ipswich Road, now a private house.

Bartley argues that reformers initially aimed to eliminate prostitution, realised this would not be possible and then turned their attention to attempting to mitigate its contributory causes. She says that by 1885 there were 106 organisations set up in England to this end. The Leeds Ladies' Association, for instance, was targeting the 'poverty, neglect or evil example' that was felt to be a stepping-stone to prostitution.[27] Colchester's ladies seem to have been quick off the mark in this regard. Colchester's Refuge for Unfortunate Females in Ipswich Road was set up in 1860, just four years after the arrival of the garrison. Its instigator was the Reverend Henry Olivier, formerly curate of All Saints church. His low opinion of the character of the girls who marched with the soldiers in Magdalen Street is quoted in Chapter 5. The home, a pretty little brick and flint cottage, was a 'benevolent refuge for the fallen' built by Louisa Round and is now a private house. The 1861 census enumerator logged three women residents – the matron (Mrs Amelia Buckingham, a nurse, whose chair-maker husband lived elsewhere in the town) and two boarders (Sarah Martin, an 18-year-old shoe binder, and Sarah Wood, 21, a servant of all work). The charity was conducted by Mrs Louisa Round of Hollytrees, widow of the rector of St Runwald, and supported by voluntary contributions.[28] Like the Penitent Female Refuge supported by Reverend Seaman, it aimed to take in prostitutes willing to be reformed and to send them on to a variety of rescue institutions in London. This is probably the 'Colchester Home' reported in 1866 as having admitted nine girls during the year and to have assisted a further 11.[29] In 1870, according to *Goody's Almanack*, it dealt with 109 women, claiming to have rescued all but 39. It didn't succeed with all of its inmates. Julia Collins, aged 16, a prostitute from Fingringhoe, pleaded guilty to stealing three petticoats, a print dress and other articles from the Refuge and was sentenced to 14 days' imprisonment.[30] After 20 years the home was closed for a time, before being refounded around 1886 and affiliated to the diocese in 1900.[31] The diocese already had a House of Mercy at Great Maplestead, set up by a local female benefactor in the 1860s and expanded in the 1880s to include another refuge in Witham and a convalescent home at Walton. The Maplestead home accommodated about 30 women, not all of whom were from the Essex diocese.[32]

In addition to these homes intended to rescue prostitutes, there were also a large number of initiatives aimed at preventing girls from falling into prostitution in the first place. Some of the town's wealthier citizens led by example and supported the clergy's efforts. Mrs Margaret Round spent considerable energy and money attempting some practical solutions to the problem as she saw it. As Arthur Brown explains, Colchester's Ragged School in Osborne Street was set up in 1854:

> Young people were brought in from the streets to learn or relearn elementary literacy in a religious atmosphere. Mrs Round, an Anglican and a Conservative, readily co-operated with J.A. Tabor, a Liberal and Nonconformist, no small achievement at this time.[33]

The newspaper reported the touching detail that, when the school opened, 'some few of the girls who presented themselves at the schools on the first evening were above the age of children' and, rather than turn them away, special arrangements were made to accommodate them in the hope that other females from the factory would also be attracted. More than 80 girls met at the school on Monday and Tuesday evenings and over 50 boys on Wednesday and Friday.[34]

Margaret Round was the wife of banker George Round of East Hill House, and her charitable work was extensive.[35] From 1859 for 20 years she also held an evening school for girls at her house.[36] She hosted sewing classes for the Girls' Friendly Society and the Young Women's Help Society, which provided an alternative to the beerhouse for working women. She also set up a Factory Mission in 1861 to which she added a Factory Girls' Club Room in 1879. Once a week she descended on Stephen Brown's silk-spinning factory, gathered the girls together and provided religious consolation for their lot in life. Sometimes she took a visitor with her to speak, at other times she led the meeting herself.

Figure 23. Mrs Margaret Round's orphanage at the junction of Brook Street and East Hill.

On one occasion

> the girls sang some of the hymns and pieces which they are accustomed to sing during their ordinary work, and those who for the first time heard the harmony with which the room is often rendered vocal, could not fail to have been struck with the fine voices many of the girls possessed.[37]

On another occasion the Reverend William Harrison took the stand and preached to his teenage audience on the subject of 'a good time coming', on the solace to be had from dying as a Christian.[38] Margaret Round also invited the silk factory girls to summer garden parties, giving motherly advice and encouragement backed up by hymn-singing in an attempt to improve their moral stamina. She built a small female orphanage at the junction of Brook Street and East Hill, which opened in 1868. In this establishment the girls were to be educated at the local school and then 'initiated into house work and so fitted to earn a livelihood in domestic service'.[39] In 1888 Mrs Round began another initiative, presiding over recreation rooms in the High Street where a committee of ladies took turns providing evening classes and a bible class on Sundays for 'young women employed in places of business in Colchester'.[40]

From the way her activities were reported it is easy to picture Margaret Round as lady bountiful, happy to donate money to social causes and to smile benignly over assemblies organised by someone else. But she motivated others more successfully than Reverends Seaman and Dacre, with their hectoring newspaper reports. She was involved as a subscriber in founding a girls' Industrial School in 1867 in Magdalen Street. The founder of *this* establishment was much more than a lady bountiful figure. She was Mrs Frances Bree, a doctor's wife, who may have been an example of another lady attempting to control working-class families but who also strongly believed that all girls deserved protection.[41] She wrote a letter to the *Standard* appealing for support and four years later reported her success in a letter to *The Times*.[42] Her appeal was carefully written to attract her middle-class friends. She mentioned rescuing girls aged 12 to 15 from temptation and training them to be both useful servants and good wives and mothers. Sunday school attendance was part of her package, her final inducement a new generation of honest and trustworthy servants who would not lead their employers' children astray! In addition to ticking all these boxes, Mrs Bree intended what she called her Home to be self-supporting. The girls learned how to cook, sew, make bread and take in laundry. The products of their labour she intended to sell to the Home's poor neighbours – 'working men and the sick poor', while their home-made bread was supplied weekly to regular customers whom she called 'private families'. In 1871, with Mrs Round's assistance, the Home moved to the orphanage at the foot of East Hill.[43] In her letter to *The Times* Mrs Bree reported the financial underpinning of the Industrial School, which included the fact that some of the girls made a contribution to their costs. The girls, of course, were not paid for the work they did, although they did receive board and lodging. She said, 'the school is not a reformatory, but rather intended as a help and an encouragement to any girl wishing to lead an honest life', and she attached this claim to a list of the numbers of hot dinners and washdays provided for the poor from the school. Finally she complained that *not* being a reformatory seemed to put the school at a financial disadvantage in comparison with Houses of Mercy. Although government inspectors visited the school and were complimentary, it was not eligible for a grant because it was not a reformatory. Subsequently Mrs Bree relieved the Union by boarding some pauper girls in exchange for financial assistance.[44]

For at least 25 years Mrs Bree managed the finances of her Industrial School so that over a dozen girls at a time received instruction that lasted about six months. During the time Mrs Bree was associated with it this might have produced over 500 graduates, but the claim in 1891 was for only 200 graduates. This may have been due, in part, to the difficulty of raising funds and it is clear from newspaper reports of fund-raising concerts and the like that this remained a problem for Mrs Bree. She must also have had to get involved in the normal administrative activities around appointing and supporting the school's salaried matron and organising both job opportunities for the leavers and the outreach activities of the school. She was assisted by a committee that included several doctors' wives. Mrs Bree is nowhere presented as a lady bountiful, but rather as an energetic and intelligent woman who had sympathy and understanding for the plight of working families in the town and who intended to provide a practical alternative to unemployment and prostitution.

To some extent, of course, Margaret Round and Frances Bree were self-serving, since the trained domestics who graduated from the orphanage and the Industrial School were destined to service the homes of the elite rather than to work in local factories. Nevertheless, it was a means by which some poor girls were provided with encouragement and training for a respectable occupation in a time when there was little formal provision for this and at a time when, in Mrs Bree's words, 'in this garrison town the temptations to young girls are terrible to think of'. It was a goal taken up by Colchester's Women's Help Society, whose committee, at its annual meeting in 1908, reported that 'in a town containing so large a number of factories as Colchester, the need of providing a Club where the girls and young women employed in them might spend their evenings both pleasantly and profitably was one which should appeal to all'.[45] However paternalistic and conservative this initiative may appear to modern eyes, improving the lives and the working conditions of poor women was also a distinct strand in the politics of nineteenth-century feminism, supported by men as well as women.

There was another way in which lady reformers could be seen to be self-serving. Josephine Butler, in distress after the death of her young daughter following a domestic accident, said she set out to look for 'some pain keener than my own, to meet with people more unhappy than myself'. Walkowitz notes that the Ladies' National Association Board consisted of women whose average age was 47, 36 per cent of whom were unmarried, 61 per cent of whom were childless and 15 per cent of whom were widowed, a profile that Mrs Round, Mrs Bree and many on their committees also fitted.[46] Like Josephine Butler, Colchester's lady reformers no doubt also found a certain comfort in their hard work for the poor, in the gratitude expressed by the poor families and in their sense of having made at least a small difference in the world.

This charitable provision, however, was not sufficient to cope with the numbers of prostitutes in need of assistance. In 1871 the lock hospital chaplain, Reverend Dacre, drew attention to the need for some arrangement to be made to help discharged patients 'wishful of amending their manner of life' and, having failed to raise any funds by appealing locally, he tried unsuccessfully to persuade the War Office to pay the necessary expenses. His application included his quarterly lock hospital return, which showed that just four of the 43 women listed had been sent to reformatories, two to the London Female Preventative and Reformatory Institute, one to Louisa Round's Home for Unfortunate Females and the fourth to the Maplestead House of Mercy. He said that whatever moral improvement they experienced, thanks to his weekly pastoral visits while patients, did not last, 'their repugnance to the restraint of domestic service, and incapacity of earning a livelihood from their previous unsettled life, or ignorance of any trade, leading them back to their former occupation'.[47] Perhaps, like the chaplain, Colchester's reformers felt that the lock hospital patients were a lost cause. Others plainly felt parents were to blame. An anonymous report on Louisa Round's Refuge for Unfortunate Females gave the following opinion.

> It is stated (sad fact) that mothers are in most instances the cause of their daughters going astray, both by neglect and bad example. Fathers come to the home with tears in their eyes and ask what can be done for their erring children. The experience of this asylum shows that the fault commences with the mothers in the childhood of their daughters … .[48]

As we have seen in previous chapters, exhorting reluctant fellow Christians to be more active in combatting immorality was not the only difficulty faced by parish clergy. Vestries were reluctant to set money aside for brothel closure and did not invariably support a moralising clergyman. In connection with prosecuting Benjamin Firmin's brothel in Pelham's Lane (see Chapter 8), the St Runwald vestry met in October 1871 to decide how much money they needed to raise. The assistant overseer explained that a rate of 2s 1d in the pound would pay

> the Union, Borough and other ordinary calls; but it was necessary that that provision should be made to meet the expenses incidental to the prosecution of Firmin and his wife, which were estimated at £85 and to meet which an additional 11d in the pound would be required, making the total rate 3s in the pound.

Having agreed this, the vestry passed the following resolution.

> That this meeting whilst sympathising with the Rector in his desire to prevent houses of ill-fame from existing in the parish, yet protests against the manner in which this heavy expense has been brought upon an already over-taxed parish, insomuch as Firmin's ill-doing was (according to the witnesses of the prosecution) stopped sometime before the proceedings were commenced, and he had promised to leave the parish.[49]

This suggests that the moralising rector was blamed for the threat of a substantial rate increase to pay for sorting out a problem that no longer existed. Reducing immorality was clearly not at the top of the parish's list of spending priorities. Alternatively, on moral issues, the vestry preferred to act discreetly with a nod and a wink in the right quarter.

mothers, their baptised child not labelled illegitimate in the church register because the parents had been cohabiting and intended to marry. The average age of marriage reduced by several years from the early nineteenth century and the rate of prenuptial conception doubled. As Jennifer Phegley observes, working-class courtship was more casual and free, the women earning their own money and enjoying greater freedom.[59] Emma Griffin, in her provocative book *Liberty's Dawn: A People's History of the Industrial Revolution*, has even claimed that 'chastity or sexual purity was not prized at this social level'.[60] Whether or not this was true, among the working-class neighbourhoods in Colchester such evidence as there is suggests that prostitution was tolerated only up to a point.

Most of the men who were associated with the prostitutes on our database as customers, cohabiting partners or husbands were soldiers or working men. As we saw in Chapter 4, some of them were abusive and violent. However, the general level of male violence (often associated with drinking) was significant and most assault cases dealt with in the borough court were between husbands and wives or between men. We have found some examples of working-class women complaining about prostitutes, usually in connection with a husband's activities but also as neighbours. Edith Churchyard, prostitute, was taken to court for threatening her neighbour.[61] Sarah Binks, another prostitute, was given to abusing her respectable married neighbour by swearing at her and threatening to cause her physical harm.[62] In these cases the prostitutes vigorously defended themselves, which is why they were recorded in a primary source. We have no way of knowing how many cases there may have been in which the prostitute gave ground or ceased her activities because she had been shamed by her neighbours.

However, we have already noted several occasions when the police had to deal with large crowds collecting around a prostitute in the street, and in some cases a working-class neighbourhood evidently attempted to apply this kind of shaming pressure. In 1851 the newspaper reported a 'Rough Band' disturbance that had taken place in Magdalen Street. The concept of the rough band was defined by E.P. Thompson as 'rude cacophony … which usually directed mockery or hostility against individuals who offended against certain community norms'.[63] Thompson describes this custom as having its origins in the seventeenth century and becoming a subject of interest to nineteenth-century folklorists, who identified a domestic and a public form. In *The Mayor of Casterbridge*, published in 1884, Thomas Hardy described a 'skimmington ride', which was a type of rough music aiming public disapproval at, in this case, a woman with a complicated sexual history. It seems that the public form of rough music was evident in Colchester throughout the nineteenth century, despite disapproval by the elite. It always involved a crowd of people who hooted their disapproval, sometimes also banging pots and pans or throwing missiles. The elite disapproved because the behaviour was rude and the risk to property was substantial.

After the Magdalen Street rough band disturbance the magistrates were faced by three men accused of ripping a woman's dress, but they also had to adjudicate the 'disgraceful' setting of this assault. Fifty people had assembled outside Mrs Ann Foreman's house, 'assailing it with stones and brick bats and accompanying the attack with noise and hooting'. When she ran from the house to a neighbour the mob followed 'and during the progress one struck her a severe blow on the head, and others tore nearly from her back the gown' she was wearing. A local magistrate had helped the police to quell the riot and arrest the three ringleaders. Mrs Foreman said she had been taking tea with three female friends when the riot began, occasioned by 'a number of boys congregated opposite the house, playing tin kettles and throwing large stones at the door'. Other witnesses refuted the tea drinking. A neighbour, formerly a policeman, said he saw Mrs Foreman

> with two girls much intoxicated, singing and dancing in her yard in a very indecent manner before the boys in the street – so much so that several neighbours had to call their children in. Upon seeing this, the boys collected to the number of about 100 with tin kettles &c opposite the door, and Mrs Foreman threw from the window the contents of a chamber [pot] over them; this further irritated the boys, who made the greater noise there until Mrs Foreman left the house, when they followed her.

According to the arresting constable, 'the crowd consisted of not less than 300 men, women and children, and there was a general expression of indignation on the part of the women that Mrs Foreman had been misconducting herself'. The bench dismissed the three men on the grounds of conflicting evidence, but lectured them about taking the law into their own hands: 'neither the woman's intoxication nor any other misconduct on her part was a justification of the violence which she had been undoubtedly subjected to by some in the crowd'.[64] Clearly the bench's priority was to quell riot rather than immorality.

Thirty years later, in 1881, the borough coroner dealt with an inquest on Joseph Bedwell, a brewer's drayman aged 31 who had committed suicide. When his wife Sarah attributed his death to 'getting behind with money with different people' the foreman of the jury attacked her, accusing her of having 'soldiers at her house when her husband had been away' and adding, 'I know the case very well and all I can say is that the man would have been alive today if it had not been for his wife.' At this point applause broke out, much to the coroner's dismay. The jury held out for a verdict of 'temporary insanity brought on by his wife's conduct', at which applause again had to be suppressed. Sarah was escorted home by the police to protect her from a mob of 100 people and the next night between 300 and 400 people collected at her house, hooting and shouting and burning an effigy of a soldier.[65]

Nevertheless, apart from the numbers of groups with an interest in suppressing prostitution, there was evidently also a degree of sympathy for individual prostitutes and, as we have seen, both police and magistrates expressed a certain rough compassion for them from time to time. Their companions also sometimes attempted to rescue them from the clutches of the arresting constable. The newspaper reports suggest that a few of the prostitutes were 'characters', appreciated for their cheekiness and a certain flamboyance in their demeanour and appearance. This was a factor that the solicitors sometimes turned to their advantage in court.

Conclusion
It is clear that efforts were made by private citizens to reduce the effects of prostitution on the women themselves and the challenge to public decency that their activities presented. The evidence of the response of the prostitutes' neighbours is scanty, making news only when there was a clear affront to working-class men and boys, as in the cases given above. Working-class men could usually avoid close proximity with prostitutes by choosing to frequent a beerhouse that did not welcome prostitutes as customers. In Colchester's cramped housing conditions, however, it was less easy to avoid a prostitute neighbour or workmate and no doubt working-class women had their own ways of expressing disdain, although these were rarely reported in the historical sources. The ease with which some prostitutes were able to relinquish the sex trade and revert to respectability suggests that there was a level of understanding for their plight.

The reformers were motivated to help for a variety of reasons. For some it was a practical way of exercising their Christian beliefs. In persuading ignorant young girls to live modestly and deferentially they felt they were saving souls from sin in addition to rescuing bodies from a potentially dangerous lifestyle. They did this through a gentle method of friendly tea parties, religious story-telling, prayer and hymn-singing. In some cases the girl agreed to take her chances in a reformatory rather than a prison. Some *were* reclaimed and others were helped to avoid prostituting themselves. Mrs Bree, writing about her Industrial School, said that many of the girls 'keep up a correspondence with the matron, consulting her in their little difficulties, and expressing their gratitude to her and to the institution for the benefits derived by them while under her care'.[66] This kind of social work, although denigrated by some historians as an indoctrinating agency for paternalism, provided a training ground for ladies who engaged in it at a time when their organisational abilities were not much used in the public sphere.[67] When women with property were allowed to vote in municipal elections from 1869, Colchester's eligible women did so and some later served quietly and effectively on town council committees and the Board of Guardians.

Kind-heartedness was another motivator. Some female reformers, such as Elizabeth Fry and Josephine Butler, are said to have been taken unawares by the positive response they received when they went among women imprisoned in houses of correction. This acted as a powerful motivator, encouraging them to redouble their efforts to learn the skills of persuasion and practical administration so that their success could be repeated by others.

Several decades before the suffragettes' militant antics hit the headlines, some ordinary ladies and middle-class women living in small country towns and comfortable country houses in Essex were finding ways to challenge the hegemony of men in public spaces. Most did it with intelligence and persistence and, above all, with the assistance of men who agreed with their cause. Some of them did it on the foundation of their confidence-boosting work among Colchester's prostitutes and impoverished women. In the context of our database the efforts of the reformers to rescue prostitutes were not very successful. However, in the context of a developing town and its uneducated and impoverished girls, it is likely that their work did ensure that some girls were diverted away from prostitution as a solution to their difficulties.

As we have demonstrated, the reforming initiatives were organised within a culture that generally condoned prostitution. In Colchester in this period it was obscenity, indecency and vagrancy that were not condoned and were routinely punished, while prostitution itself flourished in brothels and lodging houses all over the town. On just one occasion, stimulated by a shocking rate of venereal disease within the garrison, a short-lived campaign led by the local newspaper managed to dent the laissez-faire complacency that reigned supreme in the town (see Chapter 9). But, otherwise, Victorian Colchester responded only to national initiatives in this regard – the CDAs and the 1885 Act – that were forced upon it by the campaigning efforts of others. The *Essex Standard* faithfully recorded all kinds of initiatives and efforts made in London and elsewhere to address the consequences of rampant prostitution, but Colchester borough lacked the kind of leadership that might have accomplished meaningful improvement in the lives of poor families. Instead, well-meaning men and women chipped away at the edges, trying to lead by example and to find ways to motivate others to help. Their heroic efforts have been largely forgotten since.

Notes

1. Response of political hecklers in the crowd at a public meeting in Colchester to Miss Jessie Craigen of the National Association for the Repeal of the CDAs. *ES* 27 November 1880.
2. Bartley, *Prostitution*, p. 10.
3. The 1851 census records 32 clergymen living in the town.
4. *IJ* 18 March 1854.
5. The rector of St Nicholas' gave a 'men only' address on 'social purity' and a talk to young women on "unsuspected dangers and their safeguards". *ES* 3 October 1885.

6   *ES* 21 May 1841. The 1841 census for the small parish of St James identifies several potential houses of ill fame where single women lodged. Seaman had previously served five years at Charles Episcopal Chapel, Plymouth, where he had taken an interest in a female reformatory. *ES* 14 June 1839.
7   *ES* 4 March 1842.
8   The Board of Guardians considered a detailed letter from Reverend Seaman suggesting ways in which the 'fallen females' in the workhouse might be assisted. ERO, G/Co M9 26 February 1861.
9   *ES* 25 December 1846.
10 *ES* 25 December 1846.
11 In 1870 the Reverend G. Dacre, who was chaplain at Colchester's lock hospital, reported that of 162 women sent to the hospital in its first year of operation, 26 had been reclaimed (16 per cent). *The Times* 20 July 1870, reporting proceedings in the House of Commons.
12 *ES* 25 December 1846.
13 *Ibid.* All these individuals can be found in the census; all but one had at least one servant.
14 *ES* 21 May 1841 and 25 December 1846. Others were a little braver; a rare example is Thomas Dobson's letter (Figure 2) headlined THE INCREASE OF IMMORALITY IN COLCHESTER about a public lecture where the Mayor presided and spoke about his wish to reduce the tide of vice and immorality. *ES* 11 December 1857.
15 Bartley, *Prostitution*, p. 32.
16 *ES* 3 June 1857.
17 *ES* 30 October 1874.
18 *ES* 6 April 1895.
19 *ES* 30 March and 6 April 1895.
20 *ES* 17 March 1858.
21 Twenty-first annual account of Colchester Town Mission's work. *ES* 17 April 1861. *Goody's Almanack* for 1876 reported that the Mission Hall was directed by J. Bawtree, who invited local preachers.
22 Her obituary was printed in *ES* 28 August 1886.
23 *ES* 31 August 1877.
24 *ES* 17 May 1878.
25 *ES* 24 March 1894.
26 The secretary was Sophia Eisdell and the treasurer Mary Benham, widow of the *Standard*'s editor. *ES* 12 January 1895.
27 Bartley, *Prostitution*, p. 74.
28 By her will, proved in 1887, Mrs Louisa Round made bequests to Colchester hospital and other local charities and left £1500 to the rector and churchwardens of St James, the income to be used for the infant school, the Sunday school and clothing for the poor.
29 *ES* 25 April 1866.
30 *ES* 18 September 1863.
31 ERO, D/CAc 12/13/2/8 & /1.
32 *ES* 13 December 1867 and 23 June 1888.
33 Mr Tabor was a long-serving magistrate. Brown, *Colchester*, p. 93.
34 *ES* 15 November 1854. The factory referred to was one of the town's silk-spinning factories.
35 The death of her husband aged 54 was reported in *ES* 10 July 1857.
36 *Victoria County History*, vol. 9, p. 361. In 1878 the diocese added a Lodge on East Hill to its portfolio under the auspices of the Young Woman's Help Society. Its purpose was to provide a cheap lodging house for out-of-work female servants who could provide a certificate of character.
37 *ES* 2 April 1862.
38 *ES* 2 May 1862.
39 *ES* 1 May 1868.
40 *ES* 21 January 1888.

41 Moore debates the middle-class control aspect and argues that increasing interest in child protection led to the acceptance of a child's *right* to protection. M. Moore, 'Social Control or Protection of the Child? The Debates on the Industrial Schools Acts 1857–1894', *Journal of Family* History, 33/4 (2008), pp. 359–87. Bartley, *Prostitution*, p. 168; Walkowitz, *Prostitution and Victorian Society*, p. 131.
42 *ES* 26 September 1866; *The Times* 27 January 1871.
43 In 1894 it attracted the bench's attention when the matron complained that a young vagrant they had sent to her 'is always singing in the back yard'. The mayor innocently gave the opinion that singing was 'one of the best signs of a happy home', but he did not enquire which particular song the girl had been singing!
44 *ES* 8 January 1873.
45 *ES* 7 March 1908. The Salvation Army was another group that was interested in pursuing this work once it became established in Colchester in 1882.
46 Walkowitz, *Prostitution and Victorian Society*, pp. 118–19.
47 HC/CL/JO/10: correspondence relating to the Colchester Lock Hospital, House of Commons Unprinted Papers Collection 25 May 1871. Brown, *Colchester*, p. 93.
48 *ES* 28 October 1864.
49 *ES* 13 October 1871. Defending solicitor Mr Jones claimed he had paid the Firmins' bail himself 'to save St Runwald's the expense'. *ES* 15 December 1871. Census records show that Ben Firmin was born in Fordham in 1822, so was aged about 50 in the above story. His death was recorded in Colchester 11 years later.
50 *ES* 9 June 1876. The young woman was discharged but sent to a suitable Home in Greenwich on the same day.
51 *ES* 11 February 1888. The girls were sent to an Industrial Home in Sussex and became domestic servants.
52 *ES* 8 June 1895.
53 *ES* 21 September 1866.
54 *ES* 17 June 1857.
55 *ES* 4 September 1867. After prolonged debate over several weeks the bench decided not to renew five licences while complaining that the solution was vigilance by the police and the parish, as beer houses were beyond the control of the bench.
56 *ES* 6 April 1895.
57 John 8:11.
58 Gillis, *For Better, for Worse*.
59 Phegley, *Courtship and Marriage*, chapter 2.
60 Griffin argues that, in industrialising towns, women managed to support their illegitimate children through 'a combination of abundant female employment and relatively good wages and a dense family network'. But the records of Union workhouses in Essex reveal many illegitimate children held there with or without their mothers. Griffin, *Liberty's Dawn*.
61 *ES* 8 July 1893.
62 *ES* 26 July 1890.
63 E.P. Thompson, *Customs in Common* (London, 1991), p. 467.
64 *ES* 8 August 1851.
65 *ES* 3 December 1881.
66 *ES* 27 January 1871.
67 Walkowitz, *Prostitution and Victorian Society*, pp 118-122.; Kim, 'Charitable Associations in Colchester'; K.D.M. Snell, 'The Sunday School Movement in England and Wales: Child Labour, Denominational Control and Working-class Culture', *Past and Present*, 164 (1999), pp. 122–68.

Conclusion

He says, 'my young fellows if you will enlist
A guinea you quickly will have in your fist,
Besides a crown for to kick up the dust
And drink the King's health in the morning.'[1]

This book is a local history of Colchester in the second half of the nineteenth century. But, unlike the many other local histories of the town, this is the first to consider the lives of Colchester's poor women, specifically its prostitutes. The story of prostitution has been told many times, chiefly by feminist historians and those with an interest in social welfare. The particular value of a local history of prostitution lies in the rich detail that can be amassed and woven into an account not only of the prostitutes' life cycle but also of the contest between the interlocking and competing interests that allowed the vice trade to flourish. The human story is not just the difficulty of hard lives, impoverished childhoods, overcrowded housing and insufficient incomes but also the dawning realisation in the better-off part of the community that these problems could no longer be ignored or shuffled off into the Union workhouse.

The arrival of the garrison in 1856 was the catalyst for an explosion of prostitution. We cannot assume that every town and port identified in the CDA legislation experienced a similar story to Colchester's and, without being able to research this in any depth, we have indicated where Colchester seems to have been different – in, for instance, the venereal disease statistics, the geography of prostitution and the numbers of women involved. There was evidently a mismatch between the garrison CO's responsibility for his men and the borough council's responsibility for its citizens. The CO did not confine his men to barracks and when soldiers misbehaved outside the barracks it became the town's responsibility to deal with the outcome. The town began by treating errant soldiers like errant men in general but the cost of this, both financial and in policing terms, soon became unacceptable and the police were instructed to back off and to encourage the military to police itself as far as possible. Individual soldiers moved on regularly with their regiments, leaving behind them irregular families of women and children, some of whom then became the town's responsibility. Although it was routine for the town's Board of Guardians to pursue errant fathers for the cost of maintaining their children this was not possible when the man in question was a serving soldier. On the other hand, because venereal disease was thought to be spread by women, the town got the blame for soldiers incapacitated by venereal disease but was unable legally (and was also unwilling) to restrict prostitution or to fund the women's medical care. In researching the development of this uneasy relationship between garrison and town we have presented a new local history of Colchester, one that identifies prostitution as a significant factor in the development of the town in this period.

It might be assumed that what was written about prostitution would be an expression of what was done about it – that some men would complain and others would respond effectively. But this was not the case. Vice was deplored by some but tolerated by many. The harm that it did in terms of venereal disease was hidden away in the camp hospital and the lock hospital and in a variety of euphemistic descriptions of the offspring of affected parents. However, the moral harm was less easy to ignore because prostitutes were perceived to pose a threat to men in terms of their enticements to immorality. In addition, prostitutes refused to accept the role of invisible woman, as prostitution was not a crime: a prostitute, by definition, must be visible, and Colchester's certainly were. Their visibility was assisted by the men who traded in the commodity as pimps and customers and the women who recruited prostitutes and ran brothels. This resistance to middle-class moral norms gave the men with the responsibility for dealing with prostitution a huge problem and is one explanation for the laissez-faire attitude that prevailed until the late 1880s. Other explanations were linked to the weakness of the law, the desire to encourage spending in the town while reducing expenditure on poverty and to support the local brewers and business interests, and a fastidious disinclination to engage with campaigns to improve morality.

Analysis of the database on which this book is based suggests that Colchester's nineteenth-century prostitutes were working-class girls and young women with an eye to the main chance. As women they were expected to work long and drudging days for meagre wages that were neither reliable nor sufficient to keep want at bay. For some, prostitution was part of the make-do-and-mend economy of the working-class female, helpful in topping up wages in weeks where short-time working or illness reduced income. Others used prostitution, with its additional opportunities for financial gain through theft, as their sole occupation. Some in both of these groups may have used prostitution as a route to marriage, perhaps not realising initially that marriage to a soldier was a risky choice unless permission was given by the CO.

The prostitutes who struggled because they were either very young and inexperienced or older and diseased offered a vagrant kind of prostitution where they lay with their customers in fields, ditches and sheds. For such females the only alternative to this miserable existence was the Union workhouse. For most of Colchester's nineteenth-century prostitutes, prostitution was a stop-gap solution to intolerable poverty, but once they had experienced the life many were unwilling to return to the long days of drudgery expected of servants and factory women. This was said to be their excuse when confronted with the offer of reformatory or workhouse. But it was also an excuse used by unsuccessful would-be reformers.

The men who feature in the database also used prostitutes in different ways. Some treated them with violence that broke bones and caused other severe injuries, generally as a result of a break-down in agreements initially reached between prostitutes and their clients, often complicated by the influence of alcohol. The prostitute might have felt she had solicited successfully only to find herself attacked before any money had changed hands. Or the man might change his mind and she might then shriek an insult which was excuse enough for the man to knock her down. Some men just disliked being accosted by a prostitute and felt this was provocation enough to assault her. But the majority of the prostitutes' customers completed the transaction in an orderly fashion and some clearly formed an attachment to individual women with whom they liked to spend time beyond the half hour they paid for, even including her in additional nefarious activities such as theft, receiving stolen goods and crimes involving false pretences. For soldiers unable to marry officially this was a solution to loneliness for some. Other men profited directly from prostitution by working as pimps or providing premises used as brothels.

The fact that the public house and the beerhouse were the market places for prostitution added an important dimension. As our case studies of the Ship, the Lifeboat and the Anchor show, such places were a significant element in working-class culture, an important social space at a time when domestic private space was so limited, a local exchange for swapping information and property and a site for self-expression through card playing, music and dancing. The public houses where middle-class men met and drank were different only in scale and politeness. For the prostitute the beerhouse represented an opportunity to earn money and to steal money, as many of the cases we have quoted demonstrate. Thanks to the large number of beerhouses in the town, Colchester's streets were not polluted by soliciting prostitutes, although shop-lifting and pick-pocketing women abounded, some of whom were also prostitutes. The magistrates, initially working with inadequate laws, seem to have seen the beerhouse as a general good, generating business and providing the working man with cheap entertainment. But when the entertainment involved prostitution and venereal disease and a great deal of disorderly behaviour in the streets their response was inept in the years before the CDAs and the Criminal Law Amendment Act (1885).

To conclude this complex and multi-dimensional account we present two women from the database, both of whom offer exceptional examples of this challenging lifestyle. Neither of them set out to be prostitutes, but each suffered as a result of their hopes and plans of marriage to soldiers going awry. In both cases the story was reported in a number of newspapers and we have standardised the spellings of names.

∽

One Tuesday evening in August 1856 Lieutenant Lewis of the German Rifles was sauntering along Colchester's Head Street with his quartermaster friend Mr Burden and a 'girl of loose character' when he found himself under attack. Marianne Meriton, who also went under the name of Mrs Lewis, came up behind him saying 'I've caught you at last with your — '. He turned around, and she rushed upon him and scratched his face. Shouting insults the whole way she followed him to the police station in the High Street where she was arrested for attempting to assault him again.[2]

There are many accounts in this period of women attacking both men and women in the streets of Colchester. Drunkenness was usually implicated and the victim often claimed not to know the attacker or to have been taken unawares by someone they thought was a friend. Neither of these excuses was presented in this case. The story that was told in the borough court by Henry Jones, solicitor, was very revealing of the potential hazards of taking up with a soldier in the 1850s. Mr Jones said Lewis had met Marianne, a woman of unimpeachable character, at Woolwich three years earlier, had seduced her and then attempted to 'cast her off without a friend in the world to assist her, either with advice or money'. But Marianne was not a woman to be cast off lightly. She had followed Lewis to Heligoland, an isolated island in the North Sea, where they went through a ceremony she was assured was a Lutheran marriage, and thence to Turkey, where 'he took her in ... because he was compelled'. The British German Legion, which had been hurriedly assembled to assist in Crimea, had arrived there too late for active service and returned to England in the summer of 1856. Some 2,000 of them came to Colchester, where they were encamped under canvas in the old barrack ground.[3] Marianne and Lieutenant

Lewis travelled back separately and met up in Folkestone before going to Colchester where, owing her £30 that she had borrowed for him from an aunt, Lewis attempted to disown her. When she caught up with him in Head Street a witness said she saw Marianne overtake him. Lewis 'turned round and struck defendant, who then flew at him'.[4] In this account it was Lewis who struck the first blow.

Having brought the case of assault to court it was very difficult for Lieutenant Lewis to present himself as an honourable man, especially when under Mr Jones' style of attack. He seems to have chosen to allow Marianne's unfeminine behaviour to speak for itself. He said she had 'gone by the name of Mrs Lewis, but not by his authority', denied they were married, but agreed he had given her money from time to time. The questions he refused to answer were to do with any regular financial support he had given Marianne, whether he had sought legal advice on Marianne's claims as a wife, whether he had borrowed money from her or induced her to pester her friends for loans, whether he had been 'kicked out of the East Kent Militia' and whether he had falsely accused Marianne of theft. Mr Jones then turned to matters more closely related to assault.

> Mr Jones – How many times have you assaulted this young woman and knocked her down? – I never knocked her down I swear. – Then how many times have you caught her by the throat till you have almost strangled her? – I have caught hold of her throat when she has assaulted me. – And then you have thrown her down? – She may have fallen. – Have there been frequent quarrels between you? – There have been matters between us several times but they are nothing to do with this case.[5]

This exposé caused some amusement in court, no doubt helped by Mr Jones' style of questioning, and laughter broke out again when the question of the Head Street assault was examined. When witness Louisa Bolinbroke was asked if she thought the assault was serious she replied flippantly that she had not felt the blow. Lewis's solicitor suggested that the bench might like to borrow his spectacles to inspect the visible scratches on Lewis's face. But Colchester's bench did not see the joke. No doubt they were anxious to maintain the paternalistic fiction (that women were unable to look after themselves) even though Marianne seemed well able to take care of herself. Magistrate Mr Cooke observed that although the case 'seemed to excite the risibility of some persons in court' it was the most serious case he had ever heard as magistrate. The mayor, assuming that the levity had been directed at Marianne, said, 'Considering the extreme provocation to which the unfortunate young woman had been subjected, the Bench could only dismiss the case with the greatest possible disgust'.[6]

CONCLUSION

Marianne presented herself not as a prostitute but as a discarded wife. She clearly had no future with Lieutenant Lewis but was hunting him down perhaps in the hope he would repay the money she had given him or, failing that, that she would have made a successful attack on his honour that would affect his reputation in the barracks. But her only recourse after the court case was to change her name and reinvent herself as a respectable woman worthy of her hire as a servant. After her experiences in Europe and the Crimea this cannot have been easy to accomplish. We have not been able to trace her story any further.

Eleven years later, in September 1867, a man fishing in the river Colne near Middle Mill at Colchester found that he had hooked the clothing on a submerged woman's body. He called a boy to hold on to her crinoline while he fetched help to pull her out of the water. She was carried to the Castle Inn at North Bridge to await the coroner's inquest next day.

The drowned woman's name was Ann Johnson and she was the 18-year-old daughter of a local railway worker. A respectable girl with a cheerful disposition, she had arrived in Colchester from Weeley, some 12 miles away, aged 16, to work in Frederick Noone's sweet shop in the High Street. The following summer a portion of the 57th regiment arrived at Colchester garrison from Ireland and Ann, who had left the shop to work in Hyam's tailoring

Figure 24. Middle Mill on the Colne, near North Bridge, where Ann Johnson ended her life. Mr Brown's silk-winding mill, with its tall chimney, which Mrs Round visited regularly to encourage the girls who worked there, lay behind the mill to the right.

factory in Abbeygate Street, caught the eye of a sergeant of the 57th, who seduced her and with whom she fell in love. But within months the sergeant was posted elsewhere. Ann's distressed mother told the coroner that 'she was unsettled about a young man – a sergeant, who went abroad … she was very much unsettled about him'. This suggests that Ann had been planning marriage with her sergeant and was bereft when he left Colchester for Manchester in early June without her. She immediately left Hyam's factory, perhaps unable to withstand spiteful comments from the other girls, and moved to the Gardener's Arms, a seedy establishment on St John's Green where she prostituted herself with the motherly encouragement of the landlord's wife, Sarah Sawyer, who said she 'used to give [Ann] food for assisting me when she had not money to pay for it herself'.[7]

Ann may have been naïve in falling in with Sarah Sawyer but, as a prostitute, she was successful on several levels. She earned enough money to buy dresses and jewellery and to enjoy some financial control of her life and she also earned the affectionate loyalty of at least two of her customers whose letters were found in her pocket and read out by the coroner: 'I am thinking of you my dear, and intend to do something for you, my dear love … I am always thinking of you and you only … I write these few lines from my heart … God bless you my only pet … .' Corporal Shears, one of the letter writers, who had witnessed her affair with the sergeant, had made his move as soon as the sergeant left town and was anxious to persuade Ann to leave prostitution for a servant job. The night before she drowned herself he had told her that 'if she did not go off the town, or go to service, I could not keep company with her as I was noticed very much'.[8]

Had Ann been able to transfer her trust and affection and, crucially, found a respectable job, she might yet have become an army wife with or without the CO's permission. But Ann found her short experience as a prostitute physically and emotionally burdensome. By late August she had begun to think of ending her life and confided as much to Corporal Shears. He said, 'she told me the life she was leading was a burden to her and she would destroy herself. She said it was all through him (the Sergeant of the 57th regiment) and that if her present mode of life did not kill her she would put herself out of the way.' She had been physically unwell in the week before her death, experiencing a fainting fit at the Gardener's Arms during which she was unconscious for half an hour. Afterwards she complained to Sarah Sawyer of 'a very heavy load on her chest' that she could only relieve by weeping. Perhaps she was referring to a broken heart or perhaps to the 'something else upon her mind' that she declined to discuss with Corporal Shears the last time she saw him. Perhaps she was pregnant, but, if so, the surgeon made no reference to this at the inquest. He told the coroner that she 'did not appear to be pregnant but he would not say she was not so'. Unusually, his 'loose evidence' was called into question by a correspondent to the newspaper, who wondered how he could have arrived at his conclusion that Ann had drowned herself without having undressed her body to look for evidence of violence. The surgeon had arrived late for the inquest and had been required to undertake a 'hurried and casual examination of the body, made while the jury were waiting for him'. The writer went on to suggest that a proper post-mortem examination to look for bruises and evidence of violence should have been carried out. [9]

Ann was last seen alive on the Saturday evening before she was found in the river. On that day she had spent two hours in the morning with the corporal in the Marlborough Head, when she talked of suicide. They met again in the early part of the evening for more than two hours at the Gardener's Arms and then again, unexpectedly, in St Botolph's Street, where he awkwardly tried to soothe her distress of mind by giving her five shillings. Her friend from her days at Hyam's, Esther Alston, saw her before midnight weeping in the passage at the Lord Palmerston in Abbeygate. She must then have wandered by herself in the dark down to the river. In the opinion of the surgeon, Mr Philbrick, she had been in the water only 24 hours, not three days. The jury passed an open verdict and the coroner commended the corporal for his kind-hearted attempts to help the young woman.[10]

This book began with the garrison and it ends with the garrison. The two stories related in this Conclusion contain many of the contrasting elements we have explored: first, the cultural setting of prostitution, which could condemn a woman in a work of fiction and yet, in a local newspaper, present a young prostitute in a truly sympathetic – even a romantic – light; second, the real difficulties around marriage to a soldier who might promise what he liked but who lived under orders and needed his CO's permission to marry; and, third, the economic benefits of prostitution to impoverished young women and the physical and emotional burdens it involved. Ann Johnson's story also reveals the surgeon's limited experience as exposed by an intelligent member of the public, the self-interested but apparently compassionate motivation of the brothel keeper and the significant social arena of the public house, where prostitutes worked day and night and where some drank heavily. It was also a world in which a woman could go missing for three days and not be searched for.

In contrast to Ann Johnson, Marianne Meriton comes across as a determined young woman unwilling to accept the 'seen but not heard' female role of her day. There is something heroic about her successful attack upon a soldier in the street and again in court. Ann Johnson was perhaps heroic in another way. She was not the only prostitute to drown herself in the river at Colchester, but she was the only one recorded dying for unrequited love. She was in a class apart, unable to move on, prevented from moving on by her experience of prostitution and her insight into her situation. Most young women in her position either endured their lot or managed to seize a lucky break, such as the support offered by Corporal Shears. We can imagine the readership of the *Essex Standard* and the *Essex Telegraph*, from the educated clergyman and his wife to the humble silk winder and her soldier friends, discussing these stories and each choosing very different reasons to account for the actions of both Marianne Meriton and Ann Johnson. The research on which this book is based provides the detailed context that helps us understand the lives and fates of these two women, as well those of the many other women who chose, or were forced to choose, to become prostitutes in nineteenth-century Colchester.

Notes
1. 'Arthur McBride', traditional song.
2. *ES* 22 August 1856 and *Essex Telegraph* 22 August 1856.
3. *ES* 23 July 1856.
4. *ES* 22 August 1856.
5. *Essex and West Suffolk Gazette,* 22 August 1856.
6. *ES* 22 August 1856; the *Essex Telegraph* for the same date gives a slightly more detailed report. The bench was composed of the mayor, Joseph Cooke, a wool merchant aged 60 and Samuel Green Cooke, a gentleman living in Lexden.
7. *ES* 18 September 1867.
8. *ES* 18 September 1867.
9. *Essex Telegraph* 13 September 1867.
10. *ES* 18 September 1867.

Bibliography

Acton, W., *Prostitution considered in its Moral, Social and Sanitary Aspect in London and other Large Cities and Garrison Towns*, 1st edn (London, 1858).
Addy, J., *Sin and Society in the Seventeenth Century* (London, 1989).
Anderson, O., 'The Growth of Christian Militarism in Mid-Victorian Britain', *The English Historical Review*, 86/338 (1971), pp. 46–72.
Apter, T., 'Pink and Blue', *Times Literary Supplement*, 12 March 2010.
August, A., 'How Separate a Sphere? Poor Women and Paid Work in Late Victorian London', *Journal of Family History*, 19/3 (1994), pp. 285–309.
Bartley, P., *Prostitution: Prevention and Reform in England 1860–1914* (London, 2000).
Bartley, P., *The Changing Role of Women 1815–1914* (London, 1996).
Brown, A.F.J., *Colchester 1815–1914* (Chelmsford, 1980).
Butler, J.E., *Personal Reminiscences of a Great Crusade* (London, 1911).
Chesney, K., *The Victorian Underworld* (London, 1970).
Christian, E.B.V., *A Short History of Solicitors* (London, 1896).
Cooter, R., Harrison, M. and Sturdy, S., *War, Medicine and Modernity* (Stroud, 1998).
Cox, P., 'Compulsion, Voluntarism, and Venereal Disease: Governing Sexual Health in England after the Contagious Diseases Acts', *Journal of British Studies*, 46 (2007), pp. 91–115.
Cromwell, T., *History and Description of the Ancient Town and Borough of Colchester in Essex* (London, 1825).
Crossan, C. et al., 'Excavations at St Mary Magdalen's Hospital, Colchester', *Transactions of Essex Archaeology and History Society*, 34 (2004), pp. 91–154.
Dabhoiwala, F., *The Origins of Sex: A History of the First Sexual Revolution* (London, 2012).
Davidoff, L. and Hall, C., *Family Fortunes: Men and Women of the English Middle Class, 1780–1850* (London, 1987).
Durgan, S., *Colchester, 1835–1992: An Extract from the Victoria History of the County of Essex*, vol. 9 (London, 1997).

Index

Abbeygate Street 77, 121, 194
Abbot, Sarah Ann, prostitute 64
Abell, FG, solicitor 128, 138
Acton, William 7,13, 42
Age of consent 35, 151
Alexander, Mary Ann, prostitute 114, 154
Alexander, Rebecca, prostitute 149
Alger, Elizabeth, prostitute 65
Alston, Esther 195
Anderson, Elizabeth Garrett 103
Angel Lane 58, 114
Anglican church
   Christian militarism 26
   clergy attitudes to prostitute reformation 169–71, 180
   clergy providing licen*see* testimonials 180
   clergy reformers 169, 180, 185n5
   education 4, 5, 12, 19n6, 185n5
   moralists 11, 104, 140, 148, 169, 184
   responsibility for brothel closure 4, 11, 57, 91, 135, 136, 165, 179
   Sunday school 177
   vestry resistance to brothel closure 179
Army medical services
   health statistics 98
   organisation 24
   Parliamentary Select Committee (1869) 100
   Royal Commission Report (1857) 25, 96
   soldiers' families 31n5
   venereal disease 12, 24–5, 97
Avey, Sarah, prostitute 65

Balls, Mrs, brothel keeper 43
Barker, Lucy, prostitute 180

Barn Yard brothel 42, 46, 79, 172
Barrett, Julia, prostitute 124
Bartholomew, Eva, prostitute 42
Bateman, Mary Ann, prostitute 43, 68
Bawtree, John 26
Becker, Jonathan, doctor 47
Benham, Edward, publisher 17
Benham, William Gurney, publisher 17
Binks, Sarah, prostitute 123, 182
Bird, Maria, prostitute 119
Black Boy Lane 42, 55, 75, 114, 149
Blackwell, Sarah, prostitute 89–90, 115, 116
Bolinbroke, Louisa 192
Boyden, Emma, prostitute 59
Bradnack, Samuel 21
Bree, Frances 177, 184
Brett, Samuel, brothel landlord 152–3
Bretts Buildings, brothel 80, 152, 135, 152
Brewers
   as landlords 70–71, 85
   Colchester Brewing Company Ltd. 53, 75, 153
   Daniell, Edgar 146
   Messrs Cobbold 162
   Messrs Osborne 91, 161, 165
   Messrs Stewart, Pattison & Co. 87
British Medical Journal 102, 107n5
Brittee, John, brothel keeper 75, 133
Brook Street 48, 176
Brothels
   annoyance to neighbours 57, 59, 79–80, 88
   beerhouse brothels 10, 15, 41, 70
   definition 152
   clearance 59, 80, 91, 107, 115, 120–1, 134–5, 151–4
   keepers 15, 36, 62, 69, 70, 71–2

landlords 62, 69, 70, 73, 77–9, 80, 93
rentals 153, 172
typology 41
Brown, Arthur, historian 3, 4, 11, 17, 39, 112, 150
Brown, Rev. George 172–3, 181
Brown, Lizzie, prostitute 114, 154
Bull, Rev. Edward 119
Bullock, Rev. James 180
Burlington Road 80, 121, 152
Burrows, Florence, prostitute 66
Burrows, Rosina, prostitute 43
Butcher, George, brothel keeper 87–8
Butcher, Mary Ann, brothel keeper 88
Butcher, Victoria, prostitute 77, 119
Butler, Josephine
  1871 Colchester by-election 8, 9, 41, 102, 108n37
  attitude to police 121
  campaigning 98, 102, 146
  motivation 178, 185
Butt Road 22, 24, 49, 130, 160, 163
Byford, Sarah, prostitute 88

CDAs *see* Contagious Diseases Acts
Census 18, 26, 39, 48–9, 75, 78, 88
Chapel Street 117
Chappel, Essex 56
Childwell Alley 42, 43, 46, 49, 68, 79, 83n44, 84, 88, 90, 123, 137, 152, 153
Church, JH, solicitor 153
Churchyard, Edith, prostitute 48, 51n34, 66, 182
Clark, Ishmael, pimp 43, 68, 79, 81, 157
Clover, Eliza, prostitute 77
Coe, Elizabeth, prostitute 173
Colchester borough
  annual licensing meeting 85, 87, 119–20, 135, 138, 161–6
  county court 71, 128, 140
  house of correction 3
  infectious diseases hospital 107
  jail 3, 47, 105, 180
  market 2, 31
  politics 3, 4, 5, 8, 102–3
  population 6
  public health 5, 31, 96, 111
  sessions 3, 18, 56, 69, 106, 113, 140, *see also* Magistrates

watch committee 3, 18, 113, 120
Colchester garrison
  Army Scripture Readers' Society 25, 29
  arrival 6, 15, 24, 165
  barrack accommodation 22, 24, 27
  Benevolent Institution 27
  camp school 24
  commanding officer 14, 21, 28, 32n12, 75, 96, 147, 158n27, 188, 194, 195
  development 6, 22, 188–9
  drunkenness 87
  employer of civilians 14, 31
  hospital 96, 98, 106, 146, 148, 189
  lying-in hospital 24
  picket 28, 113
  provision of diversions for soldiers 25, 26, 29, 30
  royal inspection 85
  site 22
  social events 28
  venereal disease 14, 25, 28, 67, 101, 161
Colchester Licensed Victuallers' Association 129
Colchester police force
  attitude to vice 71, 77, 91, 120, 121
  attitude to solicitors 136
  identifying brothels 78, 120–1
  identifying prostitutes 33, 35, 97
  policing criminal activity 116–22
  policing drunken disorder 12, 114, 118
  policing fights 118
  policing soldiers 15, 28, 165, 189
  professional development 15, 112–13
  taking bribes 15, 81, 121
Colchester policemen
  Appleby, PC 113
  Barton, PS 114, 119
  Bramble, PC 114
  Buen, police inspector 73, 117
  Byles, PC 121
  Coombs, head constable 115, 120–1
  Downes, head constable 69, 120, 123
  Dunn, superintendent 114–15
  Frosdick, PC 119
  Frost, Robert, PC 114
  Gentry, PS 114
  Kerridge, PC 114
  Langley, sergeant 118

INDEX

Mercer, head constable 118, 122
Neale, PC 119
Smith, inspector 115
Stannard, PC 114, 115
Stewart, Sergeant 82n12
Summons, detective 115, 117
Thorpe, PC 114
Worsley, PC 117
Colchester Poor Law Union
   Board of Guardians 4, 18, 106–7, 152–3, 172, 184, 189
   Foul ward 25, 37, 96, 98, 107, 107n7
   Outdoor relief 4, 97, 177
   Poor rate 166, 179
   Relieving officer 28, 89, 122
   Workhouse 6, 14, 27, 28, 46, 48–9, 53, 60, 69, 89, 96–7, 148, 156, 190
Colchester Women's Help Society 178
Collins, Jeremiah, pimp 152
Collins, Julia, prostitute 175
Collins, William, brothel keeper 74, 91, 92, 93n1, 153
Contagious Diseases Acts (CDAs)
   Anti-CDA campaign 81, 98, 102–4, 181
   feminist response to 8
   licensed prostitution 11, 98, 149
   policing 112, 119–20, 150–1, 191
   purpose 97
   repeal of CDAs 9, 11, 106–7, 146
   see also Legal statutes
Cook, Esther, prostitute 114
Copford, Essex 54, 58
Corbett, Rev. John 180
Cornish, Mrs Mary, brothel keeper 42, 46, 79, 83n46, 91, 172–3
Cosgrove, Mary Ann, prostitute 87
Crimea 22, 24, 191, 193
Crouch Street 3, 47, 75
Cutting, Emma, prostitute 114

Dacey, Nellie, prostitute 119
Dacre, Rev. G, lock hospital chaplain 176, 178, 186n11
Daniels, Annie, prostitute 68, 117
Darbinson, Alice, prostitute 44, 51n43
Davis, Henrietta, prostitute 88
Day, Caroline, prostitute 47, 50
Day, Ellen, prostitute 130
Deal, Cartata, prostitute 37

Dicker, Mary, prostitute 45, 50n1
Dines, Alice, prostitute 48, 139n27
Disorderly house 160, 162
Double standard 62–3, 82, 97, 102, 111
Dowsett, Elizabeth, prostitute 115, 142
Duncan, Dr, magistrate 64

Eaden, John, publican 161
East Hill 3, 176, 177
Eld Lane 65
Ellis, Eliza, prostitute 116, 119
Elmstead, Essex 41
Essex and Colchester voluntary hospital 14, 98, 106, 147
Essex Assize 134
Essex Gazette 71
Essex militia 21–2
Essex Newsman 17, 81
Essex Quarter Sessions 164
Essex Standard
   editorial comment 141, 147–8, 155, 185
   editors 16
   reporters 17, 34, 141
Essex Telegraph
   reporting style 17, 196
Evans, Eliza, prostitute 68, 82n6

Factory Lane 27
Factory Mission, Colchester 175
Fairfax Road 123
Female orphanage, Colchester 176
Ferguson, Adelaide, prostitute 117, 118
Fingringhoe, Essex 43
Firmin, Ben, brothel keeper 70, 76, 134, 179, 187n49
Fitch, Emily, prostitute 48
Ford, Phoebe, brothel keeper 142–3
Fordham, Essex 53, 187n49
Foreman, Ann, prostitute 183
Fowell, John, brothel keeper 75
Frating, Essex 48
Frost, Mary Louisa, prostitute 114
Fry, Elizabeth, reformer 185
Fryers, Emma, prostitute 42
Fuller, Sarah, prostitute 116

Game, George, brothel keeper 153
Garland, Abraham, brothel keeper 75, 145–6
Garland, Hannah, prostitute 49

Garnham, Florence, prostitute 80, 123
Garrett, Rose, prostitute 123
George, Ellen, prostitute 80
German Legion 22, 27, 44, 191
Girls' Friendly Society, Colchester 175
Golding, Mary Ann, prostitute 67, 68, 92, 116, 156
Golding, Susannah, prostitute 77
Gonorrhea *see* venereal disease
Goodwin, Ann, prostitute 66
Goody, Henry, solicitor 69, 128, 129, 136, 138, 143, 146, 162, 166
Gorman, Rebecca, prostitute 67
Gould, Ellen, prostitute 66
Grant, Maria, prostitute 36
Gray, Lily, prostitute 114, 116

Hall, Emma, prostitute 158n34
Halstead, Essex 38
Ham, Caroline, prostitute 51n24, 115, 142
Harmer, Ann, prostitute 88, 90, 116, 118
Harmer, Victoria, prostitute 40, 158n28
Harris, Annie, prostitute 83n46, 172
Harrison, Henry, publisher 17
Harrison, Louisa, prostitute 74
Hatfield Peverel, Essex 45
Head Street 3, 75, 130, 137, 162, 166, 191
Headgate 119
Heath, Susannah, prostitute 89, 94n22
Hewitt, Elizabeth, prostitute 40
High Street 2, 31, 42, 48, 76, 77, 114, 115, 117, 124, 135, 193
Hill, Emma, prostitute 68
Hines, Emma, prostitute 49
Horne, Isaac, brothel keeper 75
Howe, James, brothel keeper 180
Howe, Samuel, brothel keeper 69, 83n23, 144–5
Howes, Emily, prostitute 115
Hunter, John, brothel keeper 71–73
Hutton, Susannah, prostitute 133
Hythe, Colchester port 1, 42, 49, 84, 85, 98

Indecency
  concept of 114
  in public 28, 54, 63, 89, 119, 149, 164, 185
  sexual assault 37
Industrial School, Colchester 177–8, 184

Infanticide 46–7, 49, 51n53
Inquest 27, 40, 47, 52n56, 57, 59, 67, 83n18, 171, 183, 193, 194–5
Ipswich 27, 42, 43, 48, 55, 65, 75, 89, 169
Ipswich Journal 17
Ipswich Road 3, 123, 174
'Irish Emma', prostitute 118
Isom, Annie, prostitute 116

Johnson, Ann, prostitute 36, 40, 44, 50n8, 193–5
Jones, Ellen, prostitute 36
Jones, Henry, solicitor 69, 73, 88, 92, 121–2
  brewer clients 135
  brothel cases 34, 92, 121–2, 134–5, 180, 187n49
  defending landlords 88, 94n11, 133
  defending vice trade 133
  family 128
  licence applications 134, 162–4
  practice 130
  property owner 135–6
  prostitution cases 130–2, 191–2
Jones, HW, solicitor 53

Kennedy, John, brothel keeper 92

Ladies' National Association for the Repeal of the CDAs 102
Lambert, Kate, brothel keeper 42, 154
Lancet, The, medical journal 97
Last George, brothel landlord 135
Last William, brothel landlord 135
Lawrence, Laura, prostitute 43
Leech, Jane, prostitute 49
Legal profession 127–9
Legal statutes
  Beer Act (1830) 85
  Contagious Diseases Acts (1864, 1866, 1869) 188
  County Courts Act (1846) 127
  Criminal Amendment Act (1885) 59, 77, 112, 123, 135, 142, 151, 191
  Lord Hardwicke's Marriage Act (1753) 44, 181
  Matrimonial Causes Act (1857) 44
  Municipal Corporations Act (1835) 140
  Poor Law Amendment Act (1834) 4

INDEX

Stamp Duty Act (1819) 16
Summary Jurisdiction Act (1848) 157n6
Vagrancy Act (1824) 112, 125n28
Lexden Road 3, 28, 92, 98
Lexden Union workhouse 37, 53, 54
Lichfield, Sarah, prostitute 74, 91
Lifeboat Alley 42, 115
Lock hospital 8, 19, 22, 71, 90, 97–107, 112, 151, 156, 178, 181
  Knott, constable 120, 134
  Taylor, constable 81
London 49, 171
Longley, Mary Ann, prostitute 116
Lord Panmure (Fox Maule-Ramsay) 27, 71
Lott, Jane, prostitute 41, 47, 123

McNeal, Mrs Sarah, brothel keeper 42, 47, 153
Maidenburgh Street 42, 45, 55, 58, 59, 75, 76, 80, 117, 121, 145, 152, 154, 168
Magdalen Street 3, 42, 46, 48, 70, 74, 75, 78, 84–5, 134, 136, 142, 153, 168, 177, 182
Magistrates
  attitude to lock hospital, 105, 151
  attitude to prostitution 68, 78–9, 142–3, 155–6, 183
  bench 16, 140–2, 148, 155
  collusion with publicans 155
  licensing discussions 70, 120, 144, 145–9, 161, 162–4
  licensing responsibility 51n36
  reducing prostitution 142
  sentences for prostitutes 107, 149–51
  supporting police 115, 121
Maple, Sarah Ann, prostitute 42
'Marmalade' Emma, prostitute 117
Marrel, Sarah, prostitute 123
Marriage, James, wheelwright 64
Martin, Geoffrey, historian 11
Martin, Sarah, prostitute 174
Mayhew, Henry 7, 13, 39
Meier, Louis, brothel keeper 89–91
Meriton, Marianne 191–2
Mersea Road 67, 76, 115, 135, 142, 180

Metropolitan police 98, 105, 112–13, 119–20, 150–1, *see also* Lock hospital
Middle Mill 193
Middleborough 75
Middleton, Emma, prostitute 152
Mighton, Jane, prostitute 131–2
Military Road 22, 55, 67, 78, 92, 119, 137
Minter, William, brothel keeper 75, 133
Moore, Alice, prostitute 89
Moss, Ellen, prostitute 40
Mostyn, Rev. George 69
Munson, Rebecca, prostitute 172
Murrells, Hannah, prostitute 37, 49, 50, 53–61, 68

NSPCC 45, 48, 52n57, 129, 137, 180
Neville, Charles, brothel keeper 74, 76
Nightingale, Florence 27, 103
Nonconformity 4, 25, 77, 78, 102, 148, 169, 180–1
  Band of Hope 173
  Colchester Town Mission 173
  Colchester Female Mission 173
Norfolk, Amelia, prostitute 49
Norman, John, surgeon 163–5, 168
North Bridge 193
North Hill 3, 42, 48, 59, 121, 168
Northgate Street 42, 154
Norwich 169
Nunn, Elizabeth, prostitute 123

Olivier, Rev. Henry, 85, 174
Osborne, Eliza, brothel keeper 117
Osborne Street 3, 26, 66, 75, 82n16, 87, 168
Owen, Rev. Edward 180
Owen, Rev. LW 180

Papillon, Philip, mayor 29
Pawn shop 39, 41
Pelham's Lane 76, 134, 149, 168, 179
Pettitt, William, publican 161–2
Philbrick, Samuel, surgeon, magistrate 120, 136, 195
Philbrick, Frederick, solicitor 136–7, 139n23, 161–2, 166
Phillips, Andrew, historian 11, 16, 103, 129

Pimps 15, 53, 60, 63, 68
Pitt, Sophia, prostitute 44, 45, 51n55,
Platford, Thomas, brothel keeper 55–61, 68, 81
Platford, William, brothel keeper 57, 75, 134
Port Lane 22, 98
Poverty 4, 5, 13, 168–9, 190
Prior, Ann, prostitute 114
Prior, Asher, solicitor 78, 128, 137, 138, 139n10, 158n41, 173, 181
Priory Street 75, 143, 168
Prostitutes *see also individual names*
  age of 35
  age at death 40
  aliases 34–5
  assaulted by customers 119, 190, 192
  child neglect 15, 47, 122
  children 46–7, 48, 123–4, 126n48, 153, 154, 180
  creating crowds 66, 115, 117, 183
  demeanour 40, 116, 184
  earnings 43, 64, 80
  fighting 66, 74, 80, 89, 114, 117, 167n8
  geography of 3, 42, 70, 168
  harbouring in brothel 41, 42, 51n29, 70, 73, 76, 120, 143, 165
  infertility 46, 49
  language 12, 40, 88, 116, 123, 140
  language used to describe 13
  living a double life 39, 40, 189
  marriage 14, 44, 45
  negative attitudes to 9, 47, 59, 171, 172–3, 189
  non-judgmental attitudes to 9, 47, 79, 111–12, 137, 146, 170, 181, 184
  numbers of 33, 35, 115, 124
  parental encouragement 14, 31, 45, 47, 123, 172, 179
  parental negative attitudes 37, 42, 179
  physical appearance 18, 41
  protesting against lock hospital 104–5
  social life 14, 68, 76, 90, 148, 160, 163, 190
  victims of theft 65
Prostitution and
  assault by men 66, 68, 77, 190, 192
  assault by women 66, 74, 88, 114
  attitudes to control 12, 30, 82, 110, 168

baby farming 27, 45
brothels 41–3
civil courts 111–112
cohabitation 132
definition of 7, 13, 33, 112, 124, 169, 189
divorce 44, 46
doctor attitudes 8, 100–1, 103–4, 106
drunkenness 87, 114, 115–6
entrapment of men 12, 54, 55, 62–3, 76, 82, 92, 189
feminist ideas 7, 16, 102, 121, 151, 178, 181
gangs 41, 54–5
marriage 45, 48–9, 183
neighbour disputes 182–3
soliciting 41, 113, 119, 149
theft 41, 64, 65, 68, 77, 89, 116–17, 190
vagrancy 67, 122–4, 185
venereal disease 46, 59, 89, 94n22
Public houses and beer houses
  Abbeygate 43, 75, 120
  Anchor 74, 75, 76, 87, 91–3, 153, 190
  Artillery Arms 76
  Bath Hotel 75, 133
  Beehive 42, 121, 153
  Black Boy 118, 119
  Blue Boar 45, 58, 114
  Boar's Head 92
  Britannia 180
  British Hotel 71–3, 83n28, 158n37
  Castle Inn 193
  Clarence 75, 133, 180
  Colchester Arms 74, 85, 142
  Crown and Anchor 65, 75, 137
  Duncan's Head 75
  Gardener's Arms 36, 66, 194, 195
  George 1
  Inkerman 136
  Jews Harp 137
  Langham Hotel, 135
  Lifeboat 42, 74, 76, 85, 87–93, 115, 190
  Lord Palmerston 44, 121, 195
  Mariners 85
  Marlborough Head 195
  Marquis of Granby 42
  Mermaid 36, 76
  New Market Tavern 67
  Paddy's Goose 73, 77
  Plough Inn 64

INDEX

Queen's Arms 134
Red Cross, 85
Red Lion 1
Royal Mortar 69
Sawyer's Arms 85, 87
Ship 119, 160–6, 167n8, 190
Sir Colin Campbell 135, 139n25
Spread Eagle 75
Star Temperance Hotel 42, 91
Sun 75, 145–6
Three Cups 1, 136
Welcome Soldier 75
Wellington 75, 85, 87, 134
White Hart 1, 75
Woolpack 76
Yorkshire Grey 85

Queen Street 26, 153, 168

Radford, Eliza, prostitute 158n34
Ragged School 3, 63–4, 175
Ralling, H, printer 17
Ram, Ben, publican 161
Rape and sexual assault 37, 43, 114
Rayner, Charles, publican 161
Reformatories
    Bethnal Green Penitent Female Refuge 170
    Colchester Penitent Female Refuge 170, 174–5
    Diocesan House of Mercy, Great Maplestead 175, 178
    Home for the Friendless of Good Character, London 170
    Home for Unfortunate Females, Colchester 108n9, 123, 174, 178, 179
    London Female Preventative and Reformatory Institution 178
    Norfolk and Suffolk Female Penitentiary 169
Reformers 16, 18, 178, 181, 184–5, *see also* Nonconformity
    Ladies' National Association Board 178
    Leeds Ladies' Association 174
Reynold's Newspaper 97
Riddell, Henry, newspaper editor 16
Robinson, Esther, prostitute 45

Robinson, Rev. Frederick 180
Rough bands 182–3
Round, Rev. James 27
Round, Louisa 174, 181, 186n28
Round, Margaret 175–7, 181
Royal Eastern Counties Institute 14

Sach, Susannah, prostitute 49
St Botolph Street 64, 195
St John's Green 77, 133, 194
St John's Street 117, 160
Saunders, Emma, prostitute 131
Schell, Susannah, prostitute 172
Seaborne, John, publican 160
Seaman, Rev. Meshach 33, 98, 124, 169–72, 174, 176, 186n6, 186n8
Seargeant, John, brothel keeper 153–4
Sir Isaac's Walk 157n18
Smith, Annie, prostitute 46, 62, 82n1, 172
Smith, Charlotte, prostitute 65, 70
Smith, Mary, prostitute 47, 119
Soldiers
    financial deals with prostitutes 65–6
    income 24
    intimidating behaviour 28, 63, 82n16, 161
    permission to marry 6, 14, 26, 29
    unstable marriages 27, 44, 189–90, 191, 192–3
    venereal disease 11, 97
    wives and families 26–7, 189
Soldiers' Daughters' Home, Hampstead 37
Soldiers' Institute, Colchester 26
Solicitors *see individual names*
    business interests 129, 135–6, 137
    professional development 128, 133, 136, 138
    professional training 127
Southernwood, Ellen, prostitute 67, 123
Sparrow, Elizabeth, prostitute 90
Stainton Ellis, Rev. Robert 104, 107n1
Stanwell Street 3, 27, 43, 53, 59, 60, 65, 69, 75, 119, 120, 144
Stone, Harry, brothel keeper 154
Stratford, Essex 64
Streeter, Harriet, prostitute 123
Suffragettes 40, 105, 185,
Suicide 40, 44, 50, 67, 158n39, 183, 195

Sutton, Elizabeth, prostitute 88
Syphilis *see* venereal disease

Tabor, James, magistrate 29, 105, 127, 134, 164, 186n33
Taylor, John, newspaper editor 16–17
Taylor, Susannah, prostitute 37
Temperance societies 71, 87, 137
The Times, newspaper 24, 31, 148
Tollesbury, Essex 49
Trinity Street 75, 168
Tyler, William, brothel keeper 75

Upsall, Emma, prostitute 43
Urkmacher, Emma, prostitute 50

Vagrancy 38, 41, 49, 54, 115, 122, 157, 190
Venereal Disease
   aetiology 95–6, 101, 147–8, 189
   civilians affected 67, 95
   medical attitudes 106, 151
   medical treatment 95–6, 101
   public meeting to discuss 29
Victoria County History 11
Vineyard Street 3, 43, 46, 73, 77, 91, 119, 168

Walford, James, brothel keeper 75
Wallace, Dr Alexander, 106–7
Wass, Elizabeth, prostitute 117
Watts, Rosina, prostitute 68
Waugh, Rev. Benjamin 180
Waylen, Edward, surgeon 101, 103, 107, 108n18, 151
Waylen, William, physician, magistrate 135
Webb, Mary Ann, prostitute 44

Weeley, Essex 193
Went, Georgina, prostitute 48, 150
West, Hannah, prostitute 114
West Stockwell Street 71, 130
Wilkins, Mrs, brothel keeper 42
Williams, Edward, physician, magistrate 101, 136, 146–8, 162
Williams, Rose, prostitute 139n23
Williams Walk 58, 59
Willis, Deborah, prostitute 46
Wilson, Ellen, prostitute 117
Wire, Charles, brothel landlord 77–9, 89, 152
Wolstenholme, Elizabeth, campaigner 102
Women's work
   age at beginning work 37
   childcare 187n60
   Hyam's tailoring factory 39, 193
   need to work 5
   silk factory 27, 38, 39, 50n12, 175, 193
   training 176, 177, 178
   wages 38– 9, 56, 80, 189
Wood, Sarah, prostitute 174
Woodford, Sarah Ann, prostitute 37
Woodham, Catherine, prostitute 157n1
Woodley, James, brothel keeper 75
Woods, Annie, prostitute 40
Working class marriage 43–6, 57, 59, 154, 181–2
Wright, Annette, prostitute 152
Wyre Street 57, 58, 75, 157n1

York, Nellie, prostitute 48
Young, Agnes, prostitute 45, 117
Young Women's Help Society, Colchester 175, 186n36
Youngs, Anna, prostitute 90